FATWAS AND COURT JUDGMENTS

Fatwas & Court Judgments

A Genre Analysis of Arabic Legal Opinion

AHMED FAKHRI

THE OHIO STATE UNIVERSITY PRESS ▪ COLUMBUS

Library of Congress Cataloging-in-Publication Data

Fakhri, Ahmed, 1949– author.
Fatwas and court judgments : a genre analysis of Arabic legal opinion/Ahmed Fakhri.
pages cm
Includes bibliographical references and index.
Summary: By examining Arabic legal opinions, Ahmed Fakhri seeks to understand how the organization of these texts accomplishes specific social goals. In doing so, he hopes to illuminate sociocultural practices among those who produce and use these texts. Like other sociolinguistics projects, this manuscript unites texts with their social contexts. Fakhri also points out that legal texts have traditionally held an important place in Arabic culture and therefore provide an especially illuminating window into the broader realm of Arabic thought and culture.
ISBN-13: 978-0-8142-1244-8 (cloth : alk. paper)
ISBN-10: 0-8142-1244-1 (cloth : alk. paper)
ISBN-13: 978-0-8142-9347-8 (cd-rom)
ISBN-10: 0-8142-9347-6 (cd-rom)
1. Arabic language—Discourse analysis. 2. Fatwas. 3. Islamic law—Language. 4. Sociolinguistics. I. Title.
PJ6074.F26 2014
340.5'922—dc23
2013030853

Cover design by James A. Baumann
Type set in Minion Pro

∞ The paper used in this publication meets the minimum requirements of the American National Standard for Information Sciences—Permanence of Paper for Printed Library Materials. ANSI Z39.48–1992.

9 8 7 6 5 4 3 2 1

to Mmiya, Nora, *and* Besma

CONTENTS

ACKNOWLEDGMENTS

The section on citations (page 91) is partly based on my 2008 article, “Citations in Arabic Legal Opinion: *’iftaa’* versus *qaDaa’*” published in D. Parkinson (ed.), *Perspectives on Arabic Linguistics,* with kind permission by John Benjamins Publishing Company, Amsterdam/Philadelphia, www.benjamins.com. The sections on rationale (page 7) and complex noun phrases (page 76) are partly based on my 2012 article “Nominalization in Arabic Discourse” published in Reem Bassiouney and Graham Katz (eds.), *Arabic Language and Linguistics,* with kind permission by Georgetown University Press. www.press.georgetown.edu.

I would like to thank two anonymous reviewers for their helpful comments and Professor Barbara Johnstone for her very encouraging feedback on an earlier version of this study. The book was partially supported by the Eberly College of Arts & Sciences Book Subvention Program.

I appreciate the professionalism of the editors and staff at The Ohio State University Press and would like to thank in particular Malcolm Litchfield, Eugene O’Connor, and Kristen Ebert-Wagner for their invaluable assistance. I also thank Dr. Martin Boyne for doing the indexes.

LIST OF TABLES

Introduction

A little more than two decades ago, an important article on the state of Arabic linguistics noted the paucity of discourse analysis studies, especially compared with other fields such as theoretical linguistics and sociolinguistics (Eid 1990:26). The author described the dire state of discourse analysis research in the following terms:

> In the area of discourse analysis, I have not found anything on spoken discourse; on written discourse or texts some work is now emerging—especially that of Johnstone and Al-Batal.

Since then, however, there has been a steady increase in the number of studies that have focused on various aspects of Arabic texts, describing salient textual features such as repetition and coordination or providing discourse accounts for the use of particular linguistic elements (Johnstone 1990, 1991; Al-Batal 1990; Fakhri 1995, 1998; Khalil 2000). In spite of this growing interest in Arabic discourse, only a limited number of studies have adopted a genre analysis approach to investigate Arabic texts. Notable examples of such studies are Najjar (1990) and Fakhri (2004, 2009). Using insights from the genre analysis model proposed by Swales (1990), Najjar (1990) and Fakhri (2004) analyze the moves utilized in introductions of Arabic research articles from the field of agricultural sciences and from humanities and social sciences research, respectively. In a similar vein, Fakhri (2009) compares and contrasts research article introductions from law and humanities.

The present study extends this line of research by investigating two culturally significant genres from the domain of law: secular court judgments and fatwas, the Islamic edicts based on *sharii'a* law. Although these two genres belong to two distinct institutions, *'iftaa'* "fatwa issuing" and *qaDaa'* "judiciary," they both aim at providing legal opinions based on *sharii'a* in one case and on secular laws and statutes in the other. The study seeks to make two important contributions. First, it builds upon the limited research on Arabic genres conducted so far and highlights the usefulness of genre analysis for achieving more meaningful explorations of Arabic texts that go beyond traditional surface descriptions of textual features. In this respect, the analysis presented here not only identifies and describes important linguistic and rhetorical properties of the data considered, but also offers insightful accounts for their occurrence in terms of the purpose of the texts that contain them and the sociocultural context in which these texts are produced and utilized. Thanks to this type of inquiry, Arabic discourse analysis will be able to keep pace with developments in other fields (e.g., applied linguistics, contrastive rhetoric, and business and technical communication) that have benefitted greatly from the thriving research on genre (Paltridge 2001; Johns 2002; Swales 2004; Hyland 2007; Loi and Sweetnam Evans 2010; Stroller and Robinson 2013).

Second, the study focuses on data from the domain of law that have rarely been explored in Arabic linguistic research. Consideration of such data may potentially lead to new insights regarding the specialized language of the law and enhance the contribution of linguists to a domain that has traditionally occupied a prominent place in Arab and Islamic culture thanks to the vast scholarship in the discipline of *fiqh,* the science of law (Hallaq 2005). Studies of legal discourse in Western cultures have shown that it is characterized by the use of a technical jargon, uncommon and often archaic terms, peculiar syntactic constructions, and the prevalence of formulaic expressions (Cornu 1990; Bhatia 1993; Tiersma 1999; Mattila 2006). The present study notes similar features in the sample of Arabic texts considered. More importantly, it offers insights regarding their function such as the formulation of legal concepts through the nominalization of verses from the Quran and their role in legal argumentation (e.g., use of repetition for emphasis and syntactic complexity for argument cohesion).

Other highlights of the study include the adoption of fundamental notions and constructs from research on language use to discuss the linguistic and rhetorical properties found in the data under consideration. For example, Goffman's (1981) notion of footing and Grice's (1991) maxim of relevance are used to explain rhetorical patterns observed in the fatwas and to elucidate the multifaceted rhetorical expertise of the muftis who wrote them. Resorting to these fundamental notions allows us to capture important generalizations about language use that are applicable cross-linguistically, and to avoid peculiar accounts that fit only the current data.

Furthermore, in order to make the analysis more meaningful, copious cultural notes are provided as well as descriptions of the sociocultural and linguistic environment in which the current data have been produced. Special attention is given to the institution of *'iftaa'*, since some readers may not be familiar with it; an effort is thus made to make the description of this institution sufficiently informative without being too cumbersome.

In brief, the study focuses on culturally significant data, adopts a genre analysis approach, a greatly valued and productive type of analysis, and attempts to provide insightful accounts for the data that are consistent with fundamental understanding of language use. This line of inquiry aims at problematizing discussions of Arabic discourse, ridding it of traditional and often simplistic descriptions of textual features, and highlighting its complexity, hybridity, and richness. A study of this sort is bound to raise questions; however, it is hoped that it will spur further research of unresolved issues, some of which are outlined in the final chapter of the book.

The book comprises five chapters. The first chapter describes the purpose and the rationale of the study, elaborating on the important contribution it seeks to make regarding the advancement of Arabic discourse. It also provides a concise discussion of the main aspects of the sociolinguistic situation of Arabic intended especially for readers who are not familiar with the Arabic language. In particular, it discusses language variation, language borrowing, and code-switching. Chapter 2 presents the theoretical framework of the study, emphasizing the notion of genre as viewed in the Swales model and its application in academic and professional settings. It also describes the institutional sources of the data, the sample of fatwas and court judgments selected, and the analytical procedure adopted. Findings regarding the rhetorical structure of court judgments and fatwas are discussed in chapter 3. The regularity of rhetorical moves exhibited by the court judgments is attributed to borrowing from French, and the rhetorical variation observed in the fatwas is accounted for in terms of the nonbinding nature of the fatwas and the complex rhetorical expertise of the muftis. Chapter 4 focuses on salient linguistic features that play an important role in achieving the purposes of the texts considered. These include complex sentence structure, extensive modification in noun phrases, the ubiquity of formulaic expressions, and the linguistic means of citing previous texts. Contextual properties relevant to the production of the texts are used to account for these features. The last chapter explores important implications of the study for genre analysis and Arabic discourse research. It includes a discussion of the significance of wholesale borrowing of rhetorical patterns from

French and its impact on Arabic, the host language. Among the important consequences of this kind of rhetorical borrowing is the need to rethink the structure of legal arguments in Arabic and to integrate the borrowed modes of arguing into a comprehensive and a coherent model of Arabic legal argumentation. The chapter also explores the tension-filled sociocultural environment surrounding the issuing of fatwas and how it shapes these texts and is shaped by them. A few remarks about genre and culture and suggestions for further research are made at the end of the chapter.

Chapter One
Purpose and Rationale

One of the fundamental developments in modern linguistics is the increasing importance given to psychological and social aspects in language study, which expands the scope of linguistic inquiry beyond the more traditional focus on the description of formal properties of language. While theories such as Transformational Generative grammar view language as essentially a mental phenomenon and underscore its cognitive dimensions and what they could reveal about how the human mind works (Jackendoff 2002; Pinker 1997, 2007), other approaches focus on the social and cultural aspects of language use and highlight the benefits of language study for understanding speech communities, and their values, beliefs, motives, and attitudes toward each other and toward others (Hymes 1964; Gumperz 1971, 1982; Gumperz and Hymes 1972). The present study, which uses a genre analysis approach (Swales 1990; Bhatia 1993; Hyland 2000) in order to explore aspects of Arabic legal discourse, belongs to this latter category, since it seeks to understand how the organization of particular texts is designed to accomplish certain social goals and thus constitutes an important means for gaining sociocultural knowledge about the producers and users of these texts. Genre analysis studies such as the present one complement other research that investigates general properties of texts, determines how these texts are put together, and elucidates phenomena such as textual cohesion and coherence. The focus of genre analysis on particular types of texts and their peculiar linguistic and rhetorical features has naturally triggered interest in understanding contextual elements that underlie these features. This linkage between text and context accounts in large measure for the appeal of genre analysis and its application in various domains of language use. The remainder of this chapter is divided into three sections. Sections 1 and 2 present the purpose and the rationale for the study and elaborate on its genre analysis foundation. A brief discussion of the sociolinguistic situation of Arabic is given in section 3, which is intended primarily for readers who are not familiar with Arabic. The phenomena of language variation, language borrowing, and code-switching are highlighted, since they will be useful for understanding later discussions.

1. PURPOSE

As indicated earlier, the purpose of the study is to investigate the rhetorical structures and linguistic features of a sample of fatwas written by various Islamic jurisconsults, *muftis,* and a sample of court judgments rendered by the Moroccan Supreme Court and to provide contextual accounts for their occurrence. Given the rarity of genre analysis studies of Arabic discourse, it is important to note that the focus of the study is the linguistic properties of the texts under consideration and *not* their content. The area of inquiry of the present study is genre analysis, which includes research on the rhetoric and language used in various disciplines such as law, humanities, and hard sciences. Swales (1990:131–32) presents a long list of textual studies of research articles in diverse fields such as engineering, biological sciences, astrophysics, and medicine. These studies conducted by linguists focus on language use and are of course not concerned with the scientific content of the articles (e.g., the behavior of certain types of cells in biology or the identification of efficient treatment of particular diseases). Similarly, the present study is about the language of court judgments and fatwas and is not a treatise on legal issues or *sharii'a* doctrine; references to content or to features of the institutions of *'iftaa'* and *qaDaa'* aim essentially to elucidate rhetorical and linguistic phenomena and to identify the motives and belief systems of the authors of the texts considered.

The specific purpose of the study is to address two main questions:

(a) What are the rhetorical moves and linguistic features that characterize Arabic fatwas and court judgments?

(b) To what extent and in what way are these moves and features motivated by the purpose of the texts considered, the characteristics of the various participants, and the sociocultural and institutional context of their production and use?

In order to address these questions in a comprehensive manner, the study draws upon relevant research on genre analysis (Swales 1990; Najjar 1990; Bhatia 1993; Duszak 1994; Paltridge 1997; Devitt 2004; Fakhri 2004; Loi and Sweetnam Evans 2010; Stroller and Robinson 2013) and legal discourse (Bhatia 1993; Cornu 1990; Feteris 1999; Tiersma 1999; Conley and O'Barr

2005; Mattila 2006; Fakhri 2009). These studies show to various degrees the benefits of analyses such as the ones proposed in (a) and (b) above for understanding properties of genres and through them the distinctive characteristics of discourse communities and cultures that utilize these genres. For example, the move analysis used in Duszak (1994:291) to explore the structure of research article introductions reveals interesting aspects of the "intellectual styles" of English and Polish researchers and shows differences between the two groups regarding "the scope of information that is normally revealed in initiating a paper and the rhetorical work that is done to handle academic face-phenomena." In his analysis of the moves that appear in job application letters, Bhatia (1993:68–75) is able to identify sociocultural factors that influence the realization of the genre: applicants from South Asia tend to use a strategy of "self-degradation," which serves "to magnify economic and social distance between the participants involved in the negotiation process." Presumably, such a strategy is intended to invoke compassion toward job applicants and, consequently, enhances the persuasiveness of the job application. Move analysis has also been useful in investigating the medical leaflets that serve to inform patients about the characteristics of particular drugs and the ways they are to be taken (Clerehan and Buchbinder 2006). The study points out how the quality of information provided in the leaflets can be improved by analyzing their generic structure and assessing its suitability. It highlights in particular the care with which the leaflets have to be written so as to balance the need for accurate information about the drugs prescribed and the concern to avoid alarming the patients and potentially affecting their therapy in a negative manner. Loi and Sweetnam Evans (2010) analyze the rhetorical features of Chinese articles from the field of educational psychology and find that authors avoid taking critical stances toward the work of others because such stances are face-threatening and violate Confucian values of honor and pride. These examples illustrate how genre analysis approaches yield important information regarding the values, concerns, and motives of the producers of texts and about the kinds of relations they have with their audiences.

2. RATIONALE

The rationale of the study is twofold. First, the analysis of texts from culturally significant domains such as law, which is the source of the data under consideration, contributes to understanding important sociocultural aspects of the communities that have produced them. Second, the study builds upon the relatively limited research on Arabic discourse and aims to broaden its scope. These two points are elaborated upon in turn.

2.1. The Importance of Legal Texts in Understanding Muslim Culture

Research by historians, philosophers, and jurists (Lagardère 1995; Powers 2002; Al-Jabri 2003; Hallaq 2005) has highlighted the role of legal texts and scholarship in learning about Muslim societies and understanding the development of Islamic thought. Guichard and Marin (1995:13) emphasize the importance of fatwas for the study of the socioeconomic life of Muslim communities in Medieval North Africa and Al-Andalus in the following terms:

> On verra que la variété des sujets abordés est considérable, et que ces documents suppléent dans une certaine mesure à la pauvreté archivistique du Moyen Age musulman occidental pour nous faire connaître de multiples aspects de la vie sociale d'al-Andalus et du Maghreb.
> We will see that the variety of topics addressed is considerable and that to some extent these documents compensate for the archival paucity regarding western Islam in the Middle Ages and inform us about many aspects of social life in Al-Andalus and the Maghreb.

In a similar vein, Lagardère (1995:18) points out the contribution of fatwas toward understanding the economic activities of these medieval communities:

> Des structures agraires, des modes de culture de ces communautés paysannes, ces fatwas nous informent avec la précision de document d'archives.
> Regarding agricultural systems and modes of cultivation in these farming communities, these fatwas provide information with the precision of archival documents.

The benefits of the study of Islamic legal documents are also the focus of seminal work by Powers (1990, 2002). In a very elaborate analysis of a court case from fourteenth-century North Africa, Powers (1990) convincingly demonstrates the value of these documents not only for understanding the practice of Islamic law in those communities but also for providing information about their social history and in particular the life of common folks. In addition to details about court procedures, the role of witnesses, and the evidentiary function of written documents, the texts considered are shown to "contain information about Muslim men and women living in fourteenth-century Fez and Tunis who were not prominent enough to merit an entry in the biographical dictionaries and whose existence has left no trace in the historical chronicles" and have yielded insights regarding, for instance, "family size, the ratio of males to females, and the frequency of divorce and polygyny in fourteenth-century North Africa" (Powers 1990:241). The value of considering old legal documents is also demonstrated by another study of fifteenth-century fatwas on the practice of *tawliij*, which is "an attempt by a proprietor to circumvent the Islamic inheritance rules by transferring wealth to one or more of his children by means of a gift, sale, or acknowledgement of a debt" (Powers 2002:206–28). Beyond illuminating the legal maneuvers involved, the study of such practice reveals important insights regarding people's values and relations to each other as indicated by the socioeconomic motives behind the practice of *tawliij*, namely the desire to avoid the fragmentation of family wealth and to favor certain relatives.

The study of legal texts is particularly important in Islamic scholarship because the *fiqh*, the science of law, has traditionally been viewed as central to the development of Arabic and Islamic thought (Hallaq 2001; Powers 2002; Masud, Messick, and Powers 1996; Meddeb 2003). In this respect, Al-Jabri (2003:93–94) notes that because of its high degree of abstraction and sophisticated theorizing, the *fiqh* has played an important role in Islamic culture. He writes:

> (1) lam yakun alfuqahaa’u yataqayyaduuna bi almumkini alwaaqi‘ii bal laqad dhahabuu ma‘a almumkinaati adhdhihniyya ’ilaa ’ab‘adi madaa mimmaa ja‘ala alfiqha fii aththaqaafati al’islaamiyya yaquumu bidhaati addawri taqriiban alladhii qaamat bihi arriyaaDiyyaatu fii aththaqaafati alyuunaaniyya wa aththaqaafati al’urubbiyya alHadiitha wa min hunaa ’ahammiyyatuhu bi annisbati lilbaHthi al’ipistimuuluujii fii aththaqaafati al’islaamiyya wa bi attaalii bi annisbati lil‘aqli al‘arabii.
> The *fiqh* scholars were not constrained by the "concretely possible," but they went far beyond to the "mentally possible," which allowed the fiqh to play in Islamic culture approximately the same role played by mathematics in Greek and modern European cultures, and thus its importance regarding epistemological research in Arabic and Islamic cultures and consequently regarding the Arab mind itself (my translation).

The author also points out the primacy of *‘ilm ’uSuul alfiqh* "the science of the sources of law" in Islamic scholarship compared to other disciplines. As an illustration, he points out the position on this issue of the ninth-century mathematician Al-Khawarizmi, who states that the main purpose of his book on algebra, *aljabru wa almuqaabala* (Al-Khawarizmi 1968), is to respond to the Muslim community's needs regarding issues related to inheritance, division of property, and trade. In other words, even such a fundamental discipline as mathematics is viewed as serving the discipline of law and its goals. Similarly, in his treatise on the relationship between science and religion, Al-Hajoui (2005:55) makes the point that the *'ulamaa'*, Islamic scholars, have traditionally viewed not only mathematics, which many have considered as part of *'ilm alfaraa'iD* "the science of inheritance," but other disciplines as well (e.g., medicine and land-surveying sciences) as crucial for the appropriate application of *sharii'a* law. It is therefore hoped that, in addition to its contribution to Arabic discourse research, the present study also contributes to understanding aspects of current Arabic cultural and thought patterns.[1] For instance, it will be clear from subsequent discussions that Arabic "thought patterns" as revealed particularly in the construction of legal arguments are not monolithic but quite complex given the juxtaposition within the legal discourse community of Western-inspired intellectual styles evidenced in the Moroccan court judgments and Islamic traditional ones represented in the fatwas. The consideration of this type of hybridity is crucial for understanding nowadays Arab and Muslim cultures and is in line with current views on culture such as that of Atkinson (1999:626–27), who rejects the received notion of culture as "relatively unchanging and homogeneous" in favor of a more complex view that takes into account "the cross-cutting influences that exist in and around all cultural scenes."

2.2. The Importance of the Contribution to Arabic Discourse

The importance of the contribution of the present study to Arabic discourse can be clearly shown through a brief survey of the main achievements realized so far in this area of inquiry. The survey will deal only with the literature on texts in Modern Standard Arabic (MSA), since it is these types of texts that are the focus of the present investigation and since most Arabic linguistics research has traditionally given privileged status to MSA, which is viewed as more prestigious than spoken regional vernaculars.[2] The discussion highlights in particular the qualitative contribution

1. It is worth noting that the use of authentic texts from other cultures also has the advantage of reducing potential ethnocentric biases that sometimes taint cross-cultural discussions. Authentic texts, which in a way represent voices from the target cultures, serve to guide the direction of the research, force researchers to pay attention to their most salient features, and constrain to some extent what they can or cannot say about those cultures.

2. Fakhri (2012a) includes a brief survey of discourse studies that have examined everyday social interaction in local vernaculars. These studies are Owens and Rockwood (2009) on the use of the expression *ya'nii* "I mean" in Arabian peninsula speech, Arent (1998) and Kharraki (2001) on negotiation strategies among Moroccan and Jordanian merchants and their customers during bargaining episodes which occur frequently in Arab markets, and Bassiouney (2009) on language and gender in television talk shows with particular focus on the speech of educated Egyptian women.

the study intends to make by adopting a genre analysis approach (2.2.1) and by exploring rarely studied data, namely legal texts (2.2.2).

2.2.1. *Development of Arabic Discourse Analysis: From Textual Analysis to Genre Analysis*

Purpose and Rationale

The following discussion examines key research in Arabic discourse and aims to show that, thanks to studies such as the present one, Arabic discourse analysis is in the process of undergoing a noticeable change from overwhelming applications of text analysis approaches that focus on cohesion, coherence, and text superstructure (Connor 2002:496) to a gradual adoption of genre analysis. As mentioned earlier, Arabic discourse research has initially focused on salient features that give it a distinctive quality. Lexical repetition, structural parallelism, and coordination with *wa* "and" are some of the more commonly studied features. Other studies have investigated the interface between grammar and discourse and explored the functions of particular linguistic structures such as the particles *qad* "already" and *'inna* "truly." Finally, a few studies have adopted a genre analysis approach to analyze the rhetorical organization of particular types of texts from academic or legal settings, for example. The present study is directly related to, and intends to expand, this last research area.

In her groundbreaking work on Arabic discourse, Professor Barbara Johnstone (1990, 1991) focuses on coordination, the repetition of syntactic structures, and the ubiquity of lexical couplets, which consist of two synonymous words connected with *wa* "and." Excerpts (2) and (3) taken from Johnstone (1991) illustrate lexical couplets and excessive use of coordination and repetition.

(2) a. wuDuuHun wa jalaa'un
Clarity and clarity
b. tatawalladu wa tansha'u
is born and emerges

(3) 'aaraDuuhaa fii ba'Di al-'aHwaali wa 'ayyaduuhaa fii 'aHwaalin 'uxraa wa qayyaduuhaa bi-ba'Di al-quyuudi fii ba'Di al-'aHwaali wa 'iltazamuu Hiyaalahaa siyaasata al-Hiyaadi fii mu'Dhami al-'aHwaali.
They [the leaders of England] opposed them [nationalist movements] in some cases, and endorsed them in other cases, and placed some restrictions on them in some cases, and advocated a policy of neutrality with regard to them in most cases.

The author attributes these features to oral styles that were valued in earlier developments of the Arabic language and to writers' desire to draw attention to the form of the message itself. The author also suggests that repetition serves as a rhetorical strategy for persuasion and emphasis through "accumulating and insisting" (Johnstone 1991:93).

Another set of studies have attempted to provide discourse accounts of particular linguistic devices and grammatical structures used in Arabic texts. Al-Batal (1990) explores the discourse functions of the connectives *wa* "and," *laakinna* "but," and *fa-* "therefore" and suggests that these connectives indicate thematic continuity or shifts in discourse and contribute to the effectiveness of arguments. For his part, Khalil (2000) demonstrates how particles such as *qad* and canned phrases such as *mina al-ma'ruufi 'anna* "it is known that" serve grounding functions in news discourse: *mina al-ma'ruufi 'anna* introduces background information, while the particle *qad* indicates a higher degree of grounding. Fakhri (1995, 1998) also presents discourse accounts of particular linguistic elements. The 1995 study uses Givón's (1983) notion of Topic Continuity to shed light on the use of the particle *'inna* "verily" as a topic marker and to explain the deletion of *waawu al-Haal* "while" in circumstantial clauses.[3] Fakhri (1998) describes how the choice of direct or indirect speech and the selection of reporting verbs are motivated by the writer's attitude toward the speech reported.

Finally, a few studies have adopted a genre analysis approach to Arabic discourse. As mentioned earlier, these studies represent an important topical shift from the analysis of features of texts in general to the analysis of the properties of specific genres. A synopsis of these studies of Arabic

3. The claim is that Topic Continuity accounts for the grammaticality of the following sentences:

(a) jaa'a samiirun wa almaTaru yasquTu.
came Samir while the rain falls
"Samir came while the rain was falling."
(b) *jaa'a samiirun almaTaru yaquTu.
came Samir the rain falls
"Samir came (while) the rain was falling."
(c) jaa'a samiirun wa yadaahu trta'ishaani.
came Samir while hands-his shake.
"Samir came while his hands were shaking."
(d) jaa'a samiirun yadaahu tarta'ishaani.
came Samir hands-his shake
"Samir came (while) his hands were shaking."

In both (b) and (d) *waawu lHaal* (the word *wa* "while") is deleted; but (d) is grammatical whereas (b) is not. The reason is that in (d) there is a continuous topic: the referent Samir is mentioned in the first clause (*jaa'a samiirun* "Samir came") and in the second clause through the pronominal form *-hu* in *yadaahu* "his hands." Sentence (b), on the other hand, is ungrammatical because there is no topic continuity since each clause in the sentence has a different "topic" (*samiirun* "Samir" and *almaTaru* "rain"). In other words, the deletion of *wa* is allowed only when there is topic continuity.

genres will clearly illustrate the benefits of genre analysis approaches, indicating in particular how they not only elucidate the typical linguistic and rhetorical patterns in genre tokens, but, more importantly, show how these patterns are motivated by contextual factors such as the purpose of the genre and the characteristics and concerns of the members of the discourse communities that utilize the genre.

In order to investigate research article (RA) introductions in Arabic, Najjar (1990) and Fakhri (2004) adopt the model proposed by Swales (1981, 1990), which describes how English-speaking authors create a research space for themselves by describing the importance of their field, justifying their contribution, and explicitly stating the purpose and the structure of their articles. The Najjar study of introductions from the field of agricultural sciences indicates differences from the Swales model: challenges to previous research which are frequent in English academic discourse do not occur in the Arabic data. The author attributes this finding to the applied nature of research in agricultural sciences, where theoretical argumentation is deemed unimportant. Fakhri's (2004) analysis of research article introductions from the humanities and social sciences also shows that previous scholarship is rarely challenged, presumably because of the educational background of the authors and the modest expectations of an emerging discourse community.

Fakhri (2009) extends this line of research by comparing and contrasting the rhetorical properties of RA article introductions from the fields of law and humanities. Compared to introductions in the humanities, the law introductions provide more reader orientation and exhibit a higher frequency of rhetorical moves that justify the research proposed. Neither discipline, however, uses challenges to previous scholarship as a means for establishing the need for the current contribution, as discussed in the Swales model. Disciplinary tendencies and authors' characteristics, especially their educational background, are the main factors provided to account for these findings.[4]

This brief survey of key research on Arabic discourse clearly shows that the current genre analysis study contributes toward broadening the scope of this research, in particular by going beyond the traditional focus on salient textual phenomena such as frequent repetition, structural parallelism, and flowery language (Al-Jubouri 1983; Johnstone 1990; Fakhri

4. It is suggested, for example, that the authors of the legal articles have been influenced by their greater exposure to French legal rhetoric. This is clearly seen in their frequent binary division of the structure of their articles, a typical organization of French legal articles. This binary structure is, according to Mendegris and Vermelle (1996:124), motivated by the adversarial nature of judicial litigation, which involves *des intérêts qui s'opposent* "opposing interests."

1998). While such early topical focus has yielded several insights on the peculiarities of Arabic prose and has been quite useful for research in other fields such as contrastive rhetoric and applied linguistics (Connor 1996; Saʿadeddin 1989; Fakhri 1994), it has tended to occupy most of the attention of scholars in the field of Arabic linguistics at the expense of at least equally fruitful inquiries that could take advantage of more recent approaches in discourse analysis and genre analysis in particular. Furthermore, as suggested in studies of contrastive rhetoric and applied linguistics, the continued focus on "exotic" linguistic features tends to reduce the rhetorical traditions of other cultures to static patterns and distracts from their complexity, variation, and richness (Connor 1996, 2002; Spack 1997; Zamel 1997; Fakhri 2009). A similar concern is pointed out within the field of second language teaching by Kubota and Lehner (2004), who, following poststructuralist and postmodern critiques of language and culture, advocate the recognition of the complexity of language learners' rhetorical and cultural backgrounds and warn against simplistic constructions of others' rhetoric. Finally, the adoption of genre analysis in this study is consistent with recent developments in other fields. In her discussion of new directions in contrastive rhetoric, Connor (2002:496–97) points out the "natural development" of contrastive studies toward cross-linguistic comparisons and contrasts of particular genres in academic and professional settings. In the area of teaching second language writing, genre-based pedagogies are gaining ground because they empower students by teaching them about urgently needed academic genres such as research articles, book reviews, and lab reports that they are bound to encounter during their academic pursuits and beyond (Hyland 2003, 2007). In sum, the present investigation intends to nudge forward the study of Arabic discourse so as to keep pace with developments in these other areas that have greatly benefited from genre analysis approaches.

2.2.2. *Contribution to the Study of Arabic Legal Discourse*

The literature on legal language in Western cultures highlights the importance of investigating its linguistic features and the often controversial consequences of their use for efficient and fair administration of justice. What is usually in contention is the peculiar nature of such features and their opaqueness that distinguish legal language from the spoken and written language of regular nonspecialized communication. These features include technical jargon, archaic terms, and borrowings from other languages. At the level of syntax, legal language exhibits a high frequency of long and complex sentences, unusual word order, lexical doublets, and long lists of conjoined phrases (Maley 1987; Gibbons 1994; Tiersma 1999; Feteris 1999; Mattila 2006). This exceptional language use is often justified by the need for precision, conciseness, and economical packaging of information, which are claimed to facilitate communication among law professionals. On the other hand, because of its opaqueness, legal jargon is resented by nonspecialist members of the speech community who often have to resort to the justice system and find themselves overwhelmed by the complexity and oddness of its modes of communication (Tiersma 1999:203–40).

Purpose and Rationale

As expected, Arabic legal language exhibits similar exceptional linguistic features, a few of which are discussed here that serve as background for highlighting the contribution of the present study. Uncommon terms and common terms that are given special meaning are prevalent in Arabic legal writing. For instance, the words *'i'dhaar* and *tanziil* (Moroccan Supreme Court 1999:693–94) are probably unfamiliar even to educated Arabic speakers who are not law specialists. The word *'i'dhaar* is a rare term which refers to the judge's formal notification of a claim against a defendant and which is intended to give the latter an opportunity to provide any defense he may have.[5] The word *tanziil,* which ordinarily means "lowering" or "reduction," is used as a technical term in the law of inheritance and refers to the situation when a man dies and is survived by his children and his father. In this case, for the purpose of inheritance, the children take the place of their deceased father and inherit his part from their grandfather when he dies.[6] What complicates matters even more is that in addition to this original meaning, the term is used also to refer

5. Decisions by the *qadi* (Islamic judge) routinely include a phrase that insures that litigants have no further concerns and that the proceedings are complete to their satisfaction. The following is an example taken from Alabboudi (1986:31) with the verb *'a'dhara* "notify" given in italics:

> wa *'a'dhara* hadaahu allaah likullin minhumaa bi 'abaqiyat lakumaa Hujjatun ghayra maa 'adlaytumaa bih.
> And he [the judge], may God guide him, notified them [the litigants] with "Do you have any evidence other than what you have provided?"

If the answer to the question is positive, the judge then gives the litigants enough time to gather the additional evidence and bring it before him for further consideration.

6. Islamic law and jurisprudence about inheritance are particularly rich in rare "technical" terms. For example, terms such as *alkalaala* are not used outside this specialized legal domain and therefore need to be explained as is done in a fatwa by Al-Moumni (1998:127). *Alkalaala* is a situation where a man deceases and leaves no children. His estate has to be divided in specific ways: For example, if he is survived by one sister, she takes half of the estate; if he is survived by two sisters, they take one third each; if he left both brothers and sisters, the estate is divided among them in such a way that the males get twice as much as the females.

more generally to the legal practice of designating any individual as one's inheritor regardless of family ties. This is, for example, how the term is used in Article 315 of the Moroccan family code (Mudawwanatu Al'usra 2008).

Borrowing terms from other languages can be illustrated by the occurrence in Moroccan legal texts of French words such as "syndic" as in *sandiik attaswiyya alqDaa'iyya* "compulsory liquidation agent" (French: syndic de liquidation judiciaire), "police" in *buliiSat atta'miin* "insurance policy" (French: police d'assurance), or the adjective "paulienne" in *adda'watu albulyiiniyya* (French: action paulienne), a type of lawsuit.[7] Sometimes, French technical terms in Roman alphabet are simply added after their Arabic equivalent to achieve a higher certainty of reference. Thus in a legislative text dealing with compensatory damages resulting from the use of nuclear energy, the French word "radio-isotopes" is inserted after its periphrastic Arabic equivalent *'annaDhaa'iru 'ish'aa'iyyatu annashaaT* (*Al Milaf* 2005, 6:432). It is worth noting, however, that the borrowing of French terms into Arabic legal texts is not exceptional or peculiar given the long contact between the two languages, which has resulted in extensive language mixing in various communicative situations as documented in the numerous studies on code-switching and borrowing (Bentahila and Davies 1983, 1992, 2002; Heath 1989).

Syntactic complexity is also quite prevalent in Arabic discourse, as illustrated in the following excerpt from a legislative text that regulates joint ownership of real estate.

(4) yajibu 'an tuHarrara jamii'u attaSarrufaati almuta'alliqati binaqli almilkiyyati almushtaraka 'aw 'inshaa'i Huquuqin 'ayniyya 'alayhaa 'aw naqlihaa 'aw ta'diilihaa 'aw 'isqaaTihaa bimawjibi muHarrarin rasmii 'aw muHarrarin thaabiti attaariix yatimmu taHriiruhu min Tarafi mihaniyyin yantamii 'ilaa mihnatin qaanuuniyya wa munaDhDhama yuxawwiluhaa qaanuunuhaa taHriira al'uquud wa dhaalika taHta Taa'ilati albuTlaan.

All dispositions related to transferring joint ownership or establishing or transferring rights in rem on it or modifying or cancelling it must, under penalty of invalidation, be recorded in an official deed or a deed

7. According to Starck (1972:782), this type of lawsuit is brought by a creditor not against the debtor himself but against *le tiers qui a acquis des biens du débiteur, en fraude des droits des créanciers.* [It is brought against] "a third party that has obtained assets from a debtor for the purpose of defrauding the latter's creditors." This type of lawsuit has its origin in Roman law and is called "paulienne" apparently because the name of the creditor who brought the lawsuit was "Paul."

with a date certain drafted by a professional affiliated with a regulated profession legally competent to draw up contracts.

(*Al Milaf* 2003, 1:226).

What is striking about this sentence, besides its length, is the number of instances of conjoining with *ʾaw* "or" and *wa* "and" (seven in total) whose purpose is to spell out the various legal acts affecting joint ownership and how these need to be officially recorded. Such high degree of specificity and comprehensiveness is needed to protect rights in a domain that is both economically important and legally complicated, namely joint ownership of real estate, and where parties may have incentives not to always act in good faith (Tiersma 1999:63). The excerpt also illustrates the high degree of syntactic complexity that results from the appearance in legislative discourse of complex noun phrases with various types of modification.

Purpose and Rationale

While the present study includes further discussion of similar linguistic features in the court judgments and fatwas, it goes beyond surface descriptions and provides deeper insights regarding, for example, the motivation behind these features and their impact on the genre in which they appear. A couple of examples illustrating this important contribution will suffice for now, as fuller elaborations are given later (see chapters 3 and 4). The first example concerns the vocabulary of fatwas. It is shown that the use of uncommon terms in the fatwas often compels the mufti to explain and illustrate their meanings, which adds a pedagogical dimension to the genre and elucidates status inequality among the participants in this communicative event, muftis and fatwa seekers.[8]

The second example is related to the syntactic complexity exhibited by the court judgments. In addition to describing the syntactic mechanisms involved, the discussion also reveals the source of such syntactic complexity and the motivation behind it. Specifically, it is shown that the syntactic patterns used in the court judgments are borrowed from French legal discourse, since French has been used as a medium of instruction in Moroccan law faculties for decades, and that they have been maintained because they provide an efficient and convenient frame for drafting court opinions. The significance of such wholesale borrowing of a readymade rhetorical apparatus will be elaborated upon by considering sociocultural factors that have facilitated it, as well as its impact on the rhetoric of Arabic, the host language.

8. This is similar to what happens in other communicative events such as doctor–patient encounters or lawyer–client conferences, where no parity is expected and the conduct of the interaction is controlled by the professional party, who asks questions and provides explanations.

3. THE SOCIOLINGUISTIC SITUATION OF ARABIC

The sociolinguistic situation of Arabic is quite complex given that this language is spoken in a large area that extends from North Africa to the Arabian Peninsula and that it has been for a long time in contact with other languages such as Berber, French, and English, which naturally has led to a great deal of interlingual influences. Various models have been proposed to account for the extreme linguistic variation present in Arab speech communities. One of the best-known of these is Ferguson's model, which suggests that Arabic is in a state of diglossia, "a relatively stable language situation in which in addition to the primary dialects of the language . . . , there is a very divergent highly codified (often grammatically more complex) superposed variety of written literature . . . , which is learned largely by formal education and is used for most written and formal spoken purposes . . ." (Ferguson 1959:336). The superposed variety is referred to as the "high" variety and the regional dialects as the "low" varieties. The high variety or *fuSHa,* labeled "Classical Arabic" by Ferguson but referred to as Modern Standard Arabic (MSA) in current Arabic linguistic literature, is shared by all Arab societies and coexists with regional vernaculars such as Moroccan Arabic, Egyptian Arabic, and Tunisian Arabic. The MSA and the vernaculars have different functions: MSA is essentially a written variety used in education, administration, journalism, and literature, while the vernaculars are used at home and for everyday social interaction.

Other scholars have proposed more elaborate taxonomies which, at times, seem to conflate language variation and stylistic variation. Blanc (1960) suggests five different categories of Arabic: Standard Arabic, Modified Classical, Elevated Colloquial, Koineized Colloquial, and Plain Colloquial. In a similar vein, Mitchell (1986:17) advocates a language continuum that includes at one end a high-flown variety represented by written Arabic prose and at the other end the stigmatized speech of uneducated people. In the middle of this continuum is Educated Spoken Arabic with three distinct styles: formal, informal-careful, and informal-casual. The multiplicity of taxonomies and the proliferation of rather vague and ambiguous classificatory terms have created quite a bit of confusion regarding the actual state of Arabic. But perhaps a more flexible, realistic, and rather modest suggestion is that made by Holes (2004:49), who assesses the linguistic situation of Arabic in the following terms:

> The concept of Arabic as a diglossic language, if it was ever accurate, is now an oversimplification: the behavior of most Arabic speakers, educated or not, is rather one of constant style shifting along a cline at opposite ends of which

are "pure" MSA and the "pure" regional dialect, more accurately conceived of as idealized constructs than real entities. Most communication apart from the most "frozen," written as well as spoken, is conducted in a form of Arabic somewhere intermediate between these two ideals but is governed by rules nonetheless, even if we cannot yet capture the full complexity of the rules that control the combining and hybridizing of the two.

The situation of Arabic is further complicated by language variation due to factors such as ethnicity, religion, urbanization, gender, and social class. Bassiouney (2009) presents a focused and quite informative discussion of the effect of these variables on language variation and change and highlights the conceptual and methodological challenges that confront research in this area. Her review of research on the interaction between gender and phonological, lexical, and morphosyntactic variables is particularly illuminating (Bassiouney 2009:128–97). She notes, for example, that unequal access to education and professional careers may account for the fact that women use MSA features less frequently than men.

Purpose and Rationale

The differences among Arabic varieties are quite important. Regional vernaculars exhibit differences at the levels of morphology, syntax, and vocabulary, and while MSA is syntactically homogenous, it includes significant variation in vocabulary across Arabic regions. As an example of such lexical variation, Holes (2004:47) mentions that the equivalent of the term "car rental" is *kiraa' al-sayyaaraat* in Tunisia but *'iijaar al-sayyaaraat* in Cairo.[9]

One of the main consequences of language variation in the Arab communities and the exposure of their members to different varieties

---

9. The following examples from MSA, Egyptian Arabic (EA), Moroccan Arabic (MA), and Gulf Arabic (GA) further illustrate some of the differences among Arabic varieties and give the reader a general idea of their magnitude. The EA and GA examples are taken from Omar (1976:31) and Holes (1984:151), respectively.

(1) a. yajibu 'alayhaa 'an laa tatanaawala haadhaa addawaa.' (MSA)
b. laazim maa tishrab had-dawa. (GA)
c. xaS-haa matshrubsh haad ddwa. (MA)
She mustn't take this medicine.

(2) a. ghaDiba li'annanaa muta'axxiruun. (MSA)
b. zi'il 'ashaan iHnaa mit'axxariin. (EA)
c. tqallaq 'laHaqqash Hna m'aTliin. (MA)
He got upset because we are late.

Note in particular the realization of negation in (1): MSA and GA use the negative markers *laa* and *maa* immediately before the verb *tanaawala* "take" and *tishrab* "drink," while MA attaches the negative cicumfix *ma . . . sh* to the verb, giving the form *matshrubsh* "not drink." Note also the lexical differences in (2) where the three language varieties express the notion of "getting upset" through different verbs: *ghaDiba, zi'il,* and *tqallaq*.

of Arabic as well other languages is the frequent occurrence of code-mixing and code-switching. In many communicative events, participants may mix, for example, MSA and a regional vernacular and switch back and forth from one variety to the other as discussed, for instance, by Eid (1988) and Heath (1989), who studied data from Egypt and Morocco, respectively. Example (5), which is taken from Heath (1989:31), illustrates the mixing of MSA (in italics) and Moroccan Arabic (MA).

(5) *lwafd lmaghribi murakkab* mn tlata dyal l'*anaaSir*.
The Moroccan delegation is composed of three elements.

The extent of language mixing sometimes depends on the kind of register considered. Heath (1989:178) examined data from a Moroccan radio soccer broadcast and found that although the base language of the broadcast is MA, the broadcasters used a large number of MSA terms pertaining to soccer such as *ljanaaH l'ayman* "right winger" and *Haris lmarma* "goal keeper." This practice is at variance with what happens in ordinary everyday speech where Moroccans use soccer terms borrowed from French (see discussion below). MSA and vernacular mixing occurs, for the most part, in speech and only occasionally in certain types of written texts. Holes (2004:381) notes the seemingly random mixing of Egyptian Arabic (EA) and MSA in magazine articles and first-person narratives and gives as an example the hendiadys *za''alni wa 'aHzananii* "it upset me and saddened me," where the term before the conjunction *wa* "and" is from EA and the one after it from MSA. Similarly, Fakhri (1998:178) documents instances of MA reported speech in Moroccan dailies where MSA is the norm, attributing such practice to sociocultural factors. More examples are reported in Eid (2002), documenting the use of colloquial Egyptian Arabic in dialogues from a sample of stories by Egyptian women writers.

The linguistic situation of Arabic is further complicated by its contact with other languages such as Berber and French in North Africa and English in parts of the Middle East. A large number of studies have been devoted to interlingual influences between Arabic and these languages at different linguistic levels and dealt with issues such as the relationship between borrowing and code-switching, the type of morphophonological adaptations made, the categories of lexical items and phrases involved, and the syntactic constraints that operate on language mixing (Bentahila and Davies 1983, 1992, 2002; Heath 1989). Since a full-fledged discussion of these issues is beyond the scope of the present work, the following remarks and illustrations will suffice to develop an idea about relevant aspects of this language contact situation.

An important consequence of the contact between Arabic and other languages is the substantial amounts of borrowing and code-mixing exhibited by Arabic regional vernaculars. For instance, MA has borrowed a large number of French words that are frequently used in informal everyday interaction. As discussed in Heath (1989), borrowing from French into MA is particularly extensive in certain domains such as sports and automobiles. The adoption of French soccer terms is especially frequent given the popularity of this sport in Morocco. Examples of such terms are *larbit* "l'arbitre" (referee), *kufra* "coup franc" (free kick), *bit* "but" (goal). Words related to automobiles include *kalksun* "klaxon" (horn), *dimara* "démarrer" (start the engine), and *gufl* "gonfler" (inflate a tire). Heath (1989:34) also discusses numerous instances where Moroccan speakers switch from MA to French or vice versa as in (6), where the French terms are in italics. This type of code-switching seems to be more frequent in the speech of educated youths.

(6) xdamt fwahad *la société d'assurances.*
I worked in an insurance company.

It is also worth mentioning that language mixing has been shown to be an important feature of particular language genres such as song lyrics. Bentahila and Davies (2002) have studied the mixing of French and Arabic in Rai music, which has flourished in Algeria and in some parts of Morocco and discuss the symbolic and communicative value of this phenomenon in a corpus of lyrics. A possible reason for language mixing in songs, besides poetic license and the rebellious attitudes it may connote, is that it reflects casual social interaction and, as a result, adds a degree of spontaneity to the lyrics. Such spontaneity would be lost if the language of the songs were artificially "sanitized" by stripping it of French phrases that are quite common in everyday talk.

SUMMARY

This chapter has described the purpose and rationale of the study, highlighting the important contributions it seeks to make regarding the advancement of Arabic discourse analysis and the sociocultural knowledge that may be gained. The study uses a genre analysis approach to investigate the moves and linguistic features of two culturally significant genres in the domain of law: court judgments and fatwas. The analysis presented broadens the scope of research on Arabic discourse by going beyond mere descriptions of textual features and exploring generic properties of texts and their contextual motivations. The focus on legal texts, rarely studied data, enhances our understanding of the complexity of language use in legal settings, especially as the discussion encompasses linguistic and rhetorical patterns traced to traditional Islamic sources as well as Western rhetorical traditions, a consequence of the long contact between Arabic and French. The chapter also gives basic information about the sociolinguistic situation of Arabic which is intended primarily for readers who are not familiar with Arabic. In particular, descriptions and illustrations of language varieties, language borrowing, and code-switching are provided.

Chapter Two
Theoretical and Analytical Framework

The purpose of this chapter is twofold. First, it discusses relevant aspects of the concept of genre as a theoretical framework that will guide the analysis and help interpret the findings and their significance. Second, it presents the texts selected and their institutional sources and describes the analytical procedures adopted.

1. THEORETICAL FRAMEWORK: THE CONCEPT OF GENRE

The concept of genre has been used in various areas of inquiry such as folklore studies, literary theory, rhetoric, linguistics, and language teaching. Because of this, Swales (1990:33) aptly notes that "the word [genre] is highly attractive . . . but extremely slippery." Studies such as Swales (1990, 2004), Hyon (1996), Paltridge (1997), Devitt (2004), and Hyland (2007) provide comprehensive reviews of the genre approaches adopted in these disciplines and highlight differences regarding definitions, classifications, and topical emphasis. The present discussion will focus on key aspects of genre deemed most relevant to the purpose of the present study, including accounts for genre emergence and maintenance and the relative importance of form and context in genre construction (section 1.1). The discussion also highlights the Swales (1990) approach to genre and its application to language use in legal and professional settings (Bhatia 1993; Duszak 1994; Fakhri 2009; Loi and Sweetnam Evans 2010; Stroller and Robinson 2013), since this research is closest to the topical focus of the present study and thus will serve to provide insights for the analysis of the rhetorical and linguistic features of the data under consideration and the underlying factors that motivate them (section 1.2).

1.1. Fundamental Aspects of Genre

A central idea in genre theory is that genres develop as responses to recurring situations that writers and readers recognize and over time become increasingly familiar with (Devitt 2004). The association of a text type with a particular situation is maintained and reinforced over time because of the resultant efficacy. A writer who is confronted with a writing task may not need to figure out an entirely new way of accomplishing it, but may instead draw upon already existing responses to similar tasks. According to Devitt (2004:15), this "dependence of genre on intertextuality of discourse" has a facilitating effect on the craft of writing:

> If each writing problem were to require a completely new assessment of how to respond, writing would be slowed considerably, but once a writer recognizes a recurring situation, a situation that others have responded to in the past, the writer's response to that situation can be guided by past responses.

Within a particular genre the influence of previous texts on current ones does not preclude some degree of variation, since no two situations are identical, and it is only natural that texts by different writers and for different audiences may vary in detail; nonetheless these texts can still be perceived as belonging to the same genre (Devitt 2004:20). Once a genre is established, its stability and continuity are often insured by the recommendations and directions of the discourse community that utilizes it. Novice participants in a particular discourse community (Swales 1990) are urged to study, get accustomed to, and use its preferred modes of communication and text types that are routinely produced by its more expert members. In academic settings, for example, a junior scholar soon discovers and learns the genre repertoire of his or her discipline that may include such text types as the research article, the review article, the abstract, and the book review.

Regarding the place of form in the conceptualization of genre, the research cited above indicates that the importance given to the formal structures of texts varies a great deal. One view is that text structure is "genre defining" and that it should play a major role in identifying and describing genres. For the proponents of this view, genre membership is crucially dependent on the presence of obligatory structural elements that "cannot vary without consequence to their genre allocation" (Hasan 1989:108, cited in Paltridge 1997:37). On the other hand, views such as those adopted in the New Rhetoric tradition (Freedman and Medway 1994) allow for textual flexibility and downplay the importance of form in genre conceptualization, focusing instead on situational contexts and social purposes of texts. In her classical essay, Miller (1984:151) views "genre as social action," and argues that "a rhetorically sound definition of genre must be centered not on the substance or the form of discourse but on the action it is used to accomplish." A somewhat intermediary position gives some consideration to form but only as one aspect among others that characterize genre, because form alone cannot define genre, and "understanding genre entails understanding a rhetorical situation and its social context" (Devitt 2004:13).

The relationship between context and genre is quite complex and has been widely discussed because of the ubiquitous belief that context plays a prominent role in shaping language use. A variety of terms are used to talk about situational features that influence language production such as "context of situation," "context of use," "situation-types," or simply "contexts" and "situations" (Devitt 1989), and different scholars tend to concentrate on contextual factors that they deem useful for accounting for some aspect of language use in which they are interested. Devitt (1989:292) thus concludes that "virtually any element of the environment of a linguistic act can be part of the situation, can affect a discourse and contribute to its meaning," and suggests that potentially relevant elements of context include settings, participants, events, relations, and purposes. In addition to elements of the immediate environment, the cultural context encompassing people's values, beliefs, and attitudes and behaviors toward each other is also important for understanding genre, since, in a fundamental sense, it is culture that determines which communicative activities may be accomplished in generic ways (Paltridge 1997:40). The close link between genre and context—both situational and cultural—makes it possible not only to understand why particular texts are shaped the way they are, but also to reconstruct from the texts themselves elements of the context, since in Halliday and Hasan's (1989:38) terms "any piece of text, long or short, spoken or written, will carry with it indications of its context."

1.2. The Swales Approach

The Swales approach to genre as presented in the author's seminal work (Swales 1990) on the topic is selected to guide the analyses of the present study for two main reasons. First, since it originates within the field of English for Specific Purposes, it tends to be more comprehensive and eclectic than the other familiar approaches to genre such as the Systemic Functional Linguistics (SFL) approach based on Halliday's (1994) linguistic theories and the New Rhetoric approach (NR) presented in Carolyn Miller's (1984) influential article and in Freedman and Medway (1994).

While the SFL approach considers the social function of genres, it gives a great deal of importance to linguistic and rhetorical patterns that characterize particular genres. The NR, on the other hand, is less concerned with linguistic considerations but instead emphasizes the sociocultural context of genre use and views genre as essentially a form of social action that is flexible and dynamic. The Swales approach constitutes somewhat of a compromise, since it is "more linguistic than NR and more oriented to the role of social communities than SFL," to use Hyland's (2007:44) characterization. It should be noted, however, that the Swales approach, as well as the other two approaches, has been developed within the context of language teaching. Swales's emphasis on linguistic features of texts is motivated by pedagogical concerns of teaching English to nonnative speakers with obvious language needs that cannot be ignored. The discussion of these features from a genre analysis perspective allows for the presentation of grammar to students in a meaningful way by showing them how grammatical structures contribute to fulfilling the general purpose of texts.

Second, beyond its use for language teaching, the Swales model has been applied with a great deal of success to analyze linguistic and rhetorical properties of texts in various languages, scholarly disciplines, and professional settings and to identify the situational and sociocultural factors that motivate them and to describe the intellectual styles they reflect (Swales and Najjar 1987; Najjar 1990; Taylor and Chen 1991; Duszak 1994; Fakhri 2004; Clerehan and Buchbinder 2006; Flowerdew and Wan 2010; Loi and Sweetnam Evans 2010). The present study is not motivated by pedagogical concerns, although one may speculate on its potential implication for teaching Arabic for professional purposes. Instead, the current analysis of linguistic and rhetorical patterns of particular texts, court judgments and fatwas, and the explanations provided for their occurrence is intended, as discussed earlier, to expand the scope of the research on Arabic discourse by adding new insights inspired by advances in genre analysis and its wide-ranging applications. Particularly relevant applications are those done within legal settings such as Bhatia's (1992, 1993) analysis of legislative and judicial texts from the British and Asian traditions and Fakhri's (2009) investigation of law research articles in Arabic. As will be clear later, this research on professional genres is extremely useful as a source of conceptual and analytical tools for the present investigation.

The aspects of the Swales approach to genre that are most relevant to the present study and thus need to be reviewed here are the following: the role of purpose in the conceptualization of genre, the notion of discourse community, the concept of move as an analytical unit, and the generic functions of grammatical structures. The primacy of purpose in constructing genre is highlighted in Swales's (1990:58) definition of genre:

> A genre comprises a class of communicative events, the members of which share some set of communicative purposes. These purposes are recognized by the expert members of the parent discourse community, and thereby constitute the rationale for the genre. This rationale shapes the schematic structure of the discourse and influences and constrains choice of content and style. Communicative purpose is both a privileged criterion and one that operates to keep the scope of a genre as here conceived narrowly focused on comparable rhetorical action. In addition to purpose, exemplars of a genre exhibit various patterns of similarity in terms of structure, style, content, and intended audience. If all high probability expectations are realized, the exemplar will be viewed as prototypical by the parent discourse community. The genre names inherited and produced by discourse communities and imported by others constitute valuable ethnographic communication, but typically need further validation.

The role of purpose as a defining characteristic of genre stems from the view that genres are "communicative vehicles for the achievement of goals" (Swales 1990:46). For example, as a genre, a research article abstract is defined and recognized on the basis of the purpose it fulfills, namely to present a concise and accurate description of the content of the article. Similarly, in business settings, a sales promotion letter is understood primarily as a document whose purpose is to convince a potential customer to buy a product or a service (Bhatia 1993:45). The role of purpose is so important that changing the purpose of a text is bound to affect its generic status. Bhatia (1993:21) notes that modifications of purpose introduced into texts belonging to a particular genre may require further division of these texts into subgenres and cites as an example the research article and its subgenres, the survey article, the review article, and the state-of-the-art article. However, he also acknowledges that, in order to achieve particular effects on their audience and to fulfill certain private intentions, skilled writers are sometimes able to introduce subtle modifications regarding purpose without infringing on generic boundaries. The definition also highlights the role of purpose in shaping the structure and content of discourse, which accounts for the fact that texts belonging to the same genre share "structure, style, content, and intended audience." These insights about the purpose of genre will help to elucidate, for example, the generic properties of fatwas and their variation.

The notion of discourse community is crucial in understanding generic practices. The definition of genre above notes the role of discourse communities in determining and labeling their genres; but this is only one of their functions. In fact, discourse communities can be quite complex entities, as discussed in Swales (1990:21–32). The author proposes that the notion of "discourse community" applies to any group of individuals that meets these defining criteria: the group has a set of common public goals, possesses relevant expertise regarding form and content, utilizes certain communication mechanisms to exchange information, and uses specific genres and specialized terminology. These characteristics will be resorted to as necessary to assess, for example, the status of muftis, the fatwa authors, and law professionals as participants in more or less coherent discourse communities or to determine the relations between the different genres utilized by their members.

Regarding move analysis, which will be adopted to identify rhetorical patterns in the data under consideration, it has gained widespread appeal as an efficacious analytical tool mostly thanks to Swales's (1990) seminal work on research article introductions and its replication in a large number of subsequent studies with data from various languages and disciplines such as Najjar (1990), Taylor and Chen (1991), Bhatia (1993), Duszak (1994), Ahmad (1997), and Fakhri (2004). This type of analysis describes the rhetorical patterns that appear in texts in terms of moves, which represent portions of text with specific communicative functions that contribute to the global purpose of the genre. Consider for example the rhetorical patterning in research article (RA) introductions. In Swales's terms, RA introductions aim at "creating a research space" for the author. This global purpose is achieved through a number of moves that serve to establish the importance of the field, to identify the research problems that still need to be addressed, and to state how these problems will be solved in the current article. The three moves are referred to respectively as "establishing a territory," "establishing a niche," and "occupying the niche" (Swales 1990:141). "Establishing a territory" may be achieved by indicating that the topic of the current article is part of a significant research area and signaled by expressions such as the following: "Recently, scholars have been increasingly interested in . . ." Reviewing previous research and indicating some gap in it that needs be filled can serve to establish a niche. "Occupying the niche" is often done by outlining the purposes of the research proposed. These moves have been revised and refined (Swales 2004). Another example of move analysis mentioned earlier concerns the sales promotion letter, which according to Bhatia (1993:46) includes moves such as establishing credentials, introducing the offer, offering incentives, soliciting a response, and using pressure tactics. The overall purpose of these moves is to persuade customers to purchase a particular merchandise or service. However, they are not equally important. "Introducing the offer" is clearly the most crucial move, and consequently it is quite elaborate and may be divided into several submoves: offering the product or service, detailing the offer, and indicating the value of the offer (Bhatia 1993:48–49).

The literature on move analysis shows that a move can be divided into submoves and that moves can vary in terms of their length, order of appearance, obligatoriness, and reoccurrence. For example, in the sales promotion letter, "introducing the offer" is obligatory and may take several paragraphs, whereas "using pressure tactics" is limited to certain types of business and may be expressed in a single sentence (Bhatia 1993:48–58). Commenting on the variation regarding the order of appearance of moves in the RA introductions, Swales (1990:145) notes that a little under 10 percent of the time "occupying the niche" appears at the beginning of the introduction rather than in its expected third place, but he still argues for the validity of the generalization that moves occur in a particular order:

> An anomaly percentage of under 10% is well within acceptable bounds in discoursal and textual studies for, even more than syntax, discourse is a phenomenon of propensities. Discourse generalizations are permeable to exceptions, and are not consequently falsifiable by limited numbers of counter-instances.

In other words, the study of discourse aims at identifying trends, patterns, and regularities rather than categorical rules (Brown and Yule 1988). The descriptions of moves summarized here will be very valuable in analyzing the rhetorical patterns of court judgments and fatwas and subsequently in providing plausible accounts for the occurrence of these patterns. For example, in contrast to court judgments, the moves found in fatwas exhibit more variation, which, it is argued, reflects differences in degree of cohesion between the two discourse communities that utilize these genres.

Finally, the last major aspect of the approach to be considered is the linkage it establishes between form and function. Important lexico-grammatical choices are shown to be quite often motivated by generic concerns. For example, the ubiquity of nominalizations in legal genres results from the need to condense several propositions and provisions into all-inclusive statements, achieving thereby a high degree of conciseness, a very valued feature of legal writing. These types of explorations of the relation between grammar and genre are very useful because they shed light on aspects of grammar that might otherwise remain obscure, and thus complement traditional discussions of "general grammar," as suggested by Bhatia (1993:156) in the following statement:

> The explanation of the use of nominal expressions of various kinds (and perhaps also for a number of other areas of grammar) comes not so much from the general grammar of English as from the grammar of the genre in which they regularly occur. In other words, these features of grammar carry genre-specific restricted values rather than general grammatical values.

The usefulness of the generic perspectives on grammar is highlighted further by analyses that seek to demonstrate in a precise manner how linguistic devices are harnessed for the purpose of effectively realizing certain rhetorical moves. Clear illustrations of this are presented in Swales (1990) regarding the role of certain grammatical elements in the formulation of moves in RA introductions. In this regard tense/aspect choices do not seem to be motivated by the "general rules" of present-ness or past-ness, but rather by other factors such as the degree of generality of the statement made by the author or the latter's stance toward the content expressed. For example, in the first move, "establishing a territory," general centrality claims tend to be expressed in the present perfect, as in the following example: "In recent years, applied researchers have become increasingly interested in . . ." (Swales 1990:144). On the other hand, for reference to previous research in this move, the past tense is selected to express remoteness and the desire of the writer to place "the cited author's work in a chiefly historical context" (Swales 1990:154). Move 3 of RA introductions, "establishing a niche," tends to be realized through such linguistic devices as adversative sentence connectors (e.g.; however, yet, nevertheless) and negative quantifiers (e.g., no, little), as in "However, there is little research . . ." (Swales 1990:155).

More recently, an increasing number of studies have investigated the functions of various linguistic elements in particular genres, especially in academic settings. Hyland and Tse (2005) examine the interpersonal and evaluative functions of complementation with *that* as in "*we believe that* . . ." in a sample of abstracts obtained from articles and dissertations in several academic disciplines, including applied linguistics, biology, business studies, computer science, electrical engineering, and public administration. One of the most important findings of the study is that the structure considered "offers writers a rich and nuanced means of commenting on their work, highlighting their stance as the theme of the sentence to ensure readers recognize their main contribution and its significance" (Hyland and Tse 2005:137). In a similar vein, Charles (2009) investigates the discourse roles of restrictive adverbs such as *only, simply,* and *merely* in theses from political and international relations and materials science. The data analysis shows that these restrictive adverbs enable authors to portray themselves as competent members of their disciplines and to make appropriate evaluations of the research of others as well as their own.

The genre analysis approach adopted in the present study allows for similar analyses that provide a novel perspective on Arabic grammar constructions and their specific functions in the genres under consideration. For example, it will be shown that nominalization of full finite clauses is used in fatwas to convert verses from the Quran into nominals in order to create legal concepts. Such a linguistic process not only offers the mufti a useful term for his argumentation but also enables him to retain much of the authority of the original Quranic text, which is bound to enhance the persuasiveness of the fatwa.

2. ANALYTICAL FRAMEWORK: DATA AND PROCEDURE

Before presenting the sample of fatwas and court judgments selected (section 2.3) and the procedures used to analyze them (section 2.4), it is necessary to describe their respective institutional sources in order to situate them in their proper context and facilitate the interpretation of their generic features. This is particularly true in the case of the institution of *'iftaa'*, the issuing of fatwas, since it is a peculiarly Islamic institution that might not be widely known. Thus section 2.1 is devoted to *'iftaa'*, while section 2.2 provides brief remarks about the Moroccan judiciary system, particularly the Supreme Court, which is the source of the court judgments considered, and about the linguistic and educational background of members of the legal discourse community.

2.1. The Institution of *'iftaa'*

There exists vast literature on *'iftaa'* that discusses its history and the changes that the institution has undergone from the dawn of Islam to modern times (e.g., Masud, Messick, and Powers 1996; Hallaq 2001, 2005; Powers 2002). Fatwas are issued by jurisconsults called *muftis*, as a response to questions addressed to them by members of the Muslim community. Their purpose is to provide information about the position of *sharii'a* law on a wide range of issues, including personal conduct, religious rituals, family relations, inheritance, and business transactions. The questioner (*mustafti*) could be a judge challenged by a difficult or a novel case, a political entity uncertain about the legality of a particular policy in the eyes of *sharii'a*, or a private citizen who needs to know about the rituals of pilgrimage, for example, or who is concerned about the legitimacy of some activity he is about to undertake. Fatwas have been regularly compiled, and many well-known collections such as

Ibn Taymiyya's *alfataawaa alkubraa* "The Great Fatwas" (Ibn Taymiyya 2002) or Al-Wanshariisii's *almi'yaar* "The Measure" (Al-Wanshariisii 1981\1983)[1] have made important contributions to the study of the development of Islamic legal thought and the social history of Muslim communities (Lagardère 1995; Guichard and Marin 1995; Hallaq 2001, 2005; Powers 1990, 2002; see discussion in chapter 1).

Historically, *'iftaa'* has always played an important role besides *qaDaa'*, the judiciary, in the administration of justice and the regulation of community affairs throughout the Muslim world. Vogel (1996:267) highlights the complementarity of the two institutions even nowadays in countries such as Saudi Arabia, where he found that *qadis* "judges" respect fatwas by muftis such as Sheikh Ibn Baz, a preeminent Saudi mufti, and even recommend that litigants take advantage of the institution of *'iftaa'* and obtain fatwas in order to support their cases. An important function of fatwas is to mediate between abstract legal doctrine and practical issues that Muslim communities have to face. Powers (2002:9) suggests that the fatwas in Al-Wanshariisii's *almi'yaar* make it "possible to observe how the law was applied [in medieval North Africa and Al-Andalus] and to analyze the complex interplay between legal doctrine and social practice." Hallaq (2001) also stresses the role of fatwas in the development of Islamic jurisprudence, since important fatwas have often been incorporated into positive law and served as precedent in subsequent litigations. This incorporation is achieved through the processes of *talxiiS* "abridgment" and *tajriid* "stripping" whereby the fatwa is summarized and unessential elements such as names of people and places are omitted so as to extract the legal solution that may be applied in future cases (Hallaq 2001:185).[2]

Special treatises called *'adabu almufti* "mufti conduct" (Masud 1984) discuss the qualifications, ranks, and professional ethics of muftis, describe the etiquette of dealing with fatwa seekers, and give guidelines for interpreting *sharii'a* law and drafting fatwas. An independent mufti (*mustaqill*) should be able to identify relevant hadith and verses from the Quran and, using various methods of reasoning, apply them to the

1. Ibn Taymiyya (1263–1328) was a prolific mufti who tended to write elaborate fatwas with extensive citations from the Quran and hadith. Al-Wanshariisii was a fifteenth-century mufti whose collection includes several thousand fatwas by hundreds of muftis who lived in the Maghreb and Al-Andalus between 1000 and 1496 (Masud, Messick, and Powers 1996:10).

2. This is quite similar to the treatment of legal cases intended to serve as precedent in court and as pedagogical tools in law classrooms as discussed in Bhatia (1993:118). The author makes the point that legal cases are often abridged versions of court judgments and may not include original information that is legally immaterial (e.g., dates and names of places).

question before him, whereas a *muqallid* is a mufti who simply bases his answer on the dominant opinion of a particular *madhhab*, a school of thought. An important recommendation in fatwa giving is for the mufti to refrain from discussing hypothetical cases and, instead, to deal with problems that have occurred in the real world. The discourse of the fatwas should be concise and free from unnecessary digressions. Hallaq (2001:169) cites the following statement by thirteenth-century mufti Ibn Al-Salah: "The mufti must make his answer concise; it is sufficient to indicate what is permissible and what is not permissible or what is right and what is wrong" (my translation). In case of uncertainty, the mufti is advised not to engage in speculation and not to shy away from admitting that he does not know the answer to the question posed to him; otherwise he exposes himself to divine punishment.[3]

Regarding the situation of *'iftaa'* in modern times, Masud, Messick, and Powers (1996) point out, first, that the issuing of fatwas and the status of muftis have been greatly affected by important changes in legal education that have resulted from the introduction of secular curricula that compete with *sharii'a* education and challenge its traditional centrality. Nowadays, in many parts of the Muslim world, lawyers and legal scholars acquire their knowledge and skills in mainstream education systems, while *sharii'a* law instruction is often relegated to specialized institutions.[4]

Second, there has been a shift of emphasis regarding the topics addressed by modern fatwas. Because of the expansion in many Muslim communities of civil law regimes that deal with secular issues, muftis are nowadays called upon to provide guidance concerning mostly religious matters such as rituals and Quranic exegesis, although they may be solicited by particularly pious Muslims who are uncertain about, or uncomfortable with, modern issues related to banking, insurance, or family planning, for example. However, fatwas have sometimes been utilized to address topics related to particular political contexts where, for instance, they are sought for the purpose of supporting or opposing policies by governments or other entities. Examples of such fatwas are those issued after the 1990 Iraq invasion of Kuwait and the subsequent intervention

3. In spite of this charge to muftis to be concise and to the point, it will be shown that the fatwas under consideration do not adhere to this recommendation and are filled with digressions of various kinds, which raises important questions regarding the purpose of the genre.

4. A good example of such institutions is Daar Al-Hadith Al-Hassaniyya in Rabat, Morocco, which was founded in 1964 for the purpose of training scholars in Quran, hadith, and *sharii'a* sciences. The school provides undergraduate and graduate curricula sanctioned by a doctorate in these disciplines. It is worth noting, though, that its curricula also include a variety of subjects such as sociology and foreign languages (e.g., French, English, and Hebrew).

by the United States of America. One of the main questions that these fatwas have had to address is whether it is legitimate for Muslims to form a coalition with non-Muslims against other Muslims. This has led to a "war of fatwas" depicted by Haddad (1996:300) in the following terms:

> From the outset, professional muftis representing various governments issued fatwas providing Islamic validation for, and justification of, the policies advocated by their respective political leaders, buttressing them with reference to quranic text and prophetic precedent. . . . Joining the fray were independent ad hoc bodies convened for the specific purpose of providing the definitive Islamic opinion on the event.

Third, a formalization of the profession of mufti has been introduced by some governments who now appoint official preeminent muftis as is the case in Saudi Arabia, Lebanon, and Yemen (Masud, Messick, and Powers 1996:27; Messick 1996:311).[5] Mallat (1996:287) provides this description of the function of the mufti of the Egyptian Republic:

> As the head of Dar al-ifta', the grand mufti presides over a large and complex bureaucracy in which the practice of fatwa giving has taken on a greater collective and consensual character than it possessed in pre-modern times. The mufti of the Egyptian territories (*mufti al-diar al-maSriya*) is the font of ifta' in Egypt, and he commends greater respect than any other mufti in the country.

Fourth, perhaps the most important change in contemporary*'iftaa'* concerns the wide dissemination of fatwas through print (newspapers, magazines, fatwa collections), broadcast media, audio and video cassettes, and the Internet (e.g., http://www.qaradawi.net). Neil Farquhar (2009), in a short piece about the proliferation of fatwas, mentions the case of an Egyptian mufti with a "widely popular dial-a-sheikh" fatwa service who explains to him the importance of fatwas and the necessity to disseminate them through modern technology, saying that "fatwas teach people good morals" and that "we have to work with the new technology and to use it to serve religion." The various modes of dissemination of fatwas have led to changes in their discursive and linguistic features designed to accommodate massaudiences. Thus attempts are made to present the content of fatwas in a more clear fashion and to make it more accessible

5. Official fatwa issuing may vary across Muslim countries. In Morocco, for example, this task is given to *almajlis al'ilmi al'a'laa* "The Superior Council of Oulema" (religious scholars), which has a wide range of duties in the religious field. The council includes a special committee in charge of issuing fatwas; but affiliated regional councils may also issue fatwas.

by switching, for example, from formal standard Arabic to regional vernaculars during the radio broadcast of fatwas (Messick 1996:320).

2.2. The Moroccan Judiciary

As indicated earlier, the court judgments selected for the study have been rendered by the Moroccan Supreme Court,[6] which is part of a court system that includes three additional types of regular courts: the Courts of Appeals, the Courts of First Instance, and the Communal and District Courts. The new Moroccan constitution adopted by a referendum in July 2011 instituted a Constitutional Court, which, among other prerogatives, insures the conformity to the constitution of laws promulgated by the parliament (see Bulletin Officiel 5952 *bis* dated June 17, 2011). There are also three specialized jurisdictions: the Administrative Courts, the Courts of Commerce, and a rabbinical jurisdiction that handles matters concerning the personal status of the Moroccan Jewish community. The Supreme Court includes specialized chambers that deal with penal, civil, commercial, social, administrative, and personal status issues. The membership of judicial committees that render the judgments is varied, but with quite a bit of overlap, since some members may sit on more than one committee. Typically each committee includes a chief judge, four counsel judges (*mustashaaruun*), an attorney general (*mudda'ii 'aamm*), and a court clerk (*kaatibu DDabT*). The Moroccan legal system is based on laws and statutes compiled in Western style codes such as the Code of Commerce and the Code of Obligations and Contracts, with a few regulations provided in Royal Decrees (*Dahirs*). Even the rules governing marriage, divorce, and inheritance, which come largely from *sharii'a,* are compiled in the *Mudawwana,* a code of personal status and family law on which the courts have to base their decisions instead of directly referring to Quran and hadith.[7]

As a discourse community, the judges, lawyers, and other law professionals gain legal training in various law faculties throughout Morocco and in specialized institutes such as *L'Institut Supérieur de la Magistrature.* The linguistic situation in which this community and its educational institutions operate is crucial for understanding important aspects of

6. The Moroccan Supreme Court will be alternatively referred to simply as the "Supreme Court" for ease of presentation.

7. However, in the event that a new case is brought before the court which has not been covered by the *Mudawwana*, direct reference to *sharii'a*, especially *alfiqh almaaliki,* the official Islamic doctrine adopted in Morocco, may be necessary. This topic is discussed in a 2005 doctoral dissertation from Daar Al-Hadith Al-Hassaniyya (see footnote 4 above) by Omar Lamine entitled *al'amalu alqaDaa'ii almaghribii fii alqaDayaa allatii lam yunaSS 'alayhaa fii mudawwanati al'aHwaali ashshaxSiyya* [Moroccan Judicial Work on Cases Not Stipulated in the Code of Personal Status].

the genres they utilize. Because of the French protectorate in Morocco from 1912 to 1956, the influence of the French language in various socio-economic domains has been quite strong. Although today Arabic is the official language of Morocco and is clearly predominant in government and educational institutions, French continues to enjoy a privileged status as a second language as indicated by its still important role in education, business and industry, and the media.[8] The influence of French is maintained not only because of its utility in these domains, but also because of the strong ties and intense sociocultural interactions between the sizeable Moroccan community living in France and its homeland. Another relevant factor is the special effort made by the French government to preserve and develop its influence in the cultural arena as indicated, for example, by its support of French lycées that educate a significant portion of the Moroccan elites in major cities of the country.

In the domain of law the role of the French language and legal tradition is quite prominent, especially in legal education, documentation, and publishing.[9] Moroccan judges and other law professionals are trained in law faculties and institutes that provide curricula in both Arabic and French. It's worth noting in particular that in addition to regular courses in various branches of the law (e.g., civil law, penal law, business law, and legal procedure), law students receive focused instruction in legal rhetoric and communication. For example, the modules on language and communication designed by the French section of the law faculty of the University of Hassan II-Ain Chock in Casablanca include the following topics:[10] *L'organisation du texte argumentatif* "the organization of argumentative texts," *les procédés de l'argumentation* "processes of argumentation," and *travail sur les documents spécialisés* "study of specialized documents." Law students also conduct their research in both Arabic and French, as indicated by the following thesis topics investigated by students at the *Institut Supérieur de la Magistrature* between 2003 and 2005:

(a) aTTuruqu albadiilatu litaswiyyati almunaaza'aati attijaariyya
Alternative means for resolving commercial disputes

8. Moroccan radio and TV stations broadcast shows and news programs in both Arabic and French. The independent radio *Medi 1* has been conceived as a bilingual news outlet. Regarding print media, political parties, for instance, often publish dailies in both Arabic and French.

9. The linguistic situation in Morocco and its impact on the legal system is very similar to the one in Tunisia, as discussed in Mattila (2006:212–15).

10. This information is obtained from a draft proposal updating the curricula of various disciplines offered by the law school. The proposal is intended to support applications for accreditation. I thank Professor Azzedine Benseghir for providing me with a copy of this document.

(b) La protection juridique du consommateur
Legal protection of consumers
(c) Droit et pratique d'acconage au Maroc
The law and practice of stevedoring in Morocco
(Institut Supérieure de la Magistrature 2009)

Regarding legal publications, there are books, journals, and other scholarly materials easily available in both French and Arabic in libraries and bookstores. Many legal periodicals are bilingual and include a section in Arabic and a section in French. This is the case, for example, with *Revue de Droit et D'Economie* (*majallat alqaanuun wa al'iqtiSaad*) "Review of Law and Economics" and *La Gazette des Tribunaux du Maroc* (*majallat alma-Haakim almaghribiyya*) "Journal of Moroccan Courts." The same bilingual system is applied in the various legal codes such as *Code des Obligations et Contrats* (*qaanuunu al'iltizaamaat wa al'uquud*) "Code of Obligations and Contracts." Even though the Arabic and French sections in these publications are separated, there are many instances of language mixing in the texts. For example, Arabic legal essays may include several references in French as well as French glosses of technical terms. In an Arabic article on employment contracts (Moumen 2000), the author cites more than twenty French references and translates some words and phrases into French presumably to avoid ambiguity, as shown in these examples:[11] *al'iltizaam bi al'ixlaaS* (Obligation de loyauté) "obligation of loyalty" and *'adam 'ifshaa' alma'luumaat* (Obligation de discrétion) "obligation of reserve." The reverse is also true, that is, the use of Arabic terms in French texts. This is particularly the case when the subject matter involved concerns rules and concepts taken from *sharii'a* law. For example, many articles on inheritance in the French version of the Moroccan family code refer to the Arabic legal concepts of *farD* and *ta'Siib* as "Le Fardh" and "Le Taasib" as indicated in Article 335, which defines the two terms as follows:

Theoretical and Analytical Framework

> Le Fardh est une quote-part successorale déterminée assignée à l'héritier. . . . Le Taasib consiste à hériter de l'ensemble de la succession ou de ce qu'il en reste après l'affectation des parts dues aux héritiers à fardh.

> The *farD* is a fixed part of inheritance assigned to the heir. . . . The *ta'Siib* consists in inheriting the totality of the estate or whatever is left of it after assigning the parts due to the *farD* heirs.

11. These are contractual obligations intended to prohibit employees who change employment from engaging in unfair competition with their former employers or benefiting from sensitive information they gained from them.

In sum, judges and other law professionals are exposed to, and employ, both Arabic and French rhetoric. An important consequence of this state of affairs is the occurrence of interlingual influences, one of which, the borrowing of rhetorical patterns from French into Arabic texts, will be discussed later as an important element in understanding the rhetorical structure of the Arabic judgments (see chapter 3).

2.3. The Data

The data for the study consist of twenty-five fatwas and twenty-five court judgments. The topical content of both sets is similar: they deal with what is generally referred to as *mu'aamalaat,* that is, commercial and business relations and transactions. This similarity in content is intended to enhance the comparability of the two sets of data by reducing topic variation, especially in the case of fatwas, which, as mentioned earlier, cover a wide range of topics. The texts selected address questions related to sales, loans, and employment, for example. Tables 1 and 2 present the topical content of the fatwas and court judgments, respectively.

In order to control for the possible effect of any one author's stylistic peculiarities, the sources of the texts are varied. The fatwas chosen have been issued by four different muftis in addition to fatwas attributed collectively to a fatwa committee, usually composed of four muftis. Two of the muftis are well-known and quite influential: Sheikh Ibn Baz of Saudi Arabia and Sheikh Yusuf Qaradawi, who is originally from Egypt but who has served in various religious and academic institutions in Qatar (see websites binbaz.org.sa and qaradawi.net). The two lesser-known muftis are Khalil Al-Moumni of Morocco and Mahmud Abdul Hameed Al-Ahmad of the United Arab Emirates. While these two lesser-known muftis may not possess the scholarly credentials that appeal to *sharii'a* specialists, their fatwas are very appropriate for linguistic study, since they result from genuine and direct social interaction between them and regular folks keen to adhere to *sharii'a* precepts and moral code. Al-Moumni, for example, provided guidance for university students while in Oujda, Morocco, and to members of the immigrant Muslim community when he moved to the Netherlands (Al-Moumni 1998).

The court judgments have been rendered by the Commerce Chamber and the Social Chamber of the Moroccan Supreme Court and appear in three issues of the law review *Al Milaf* "The File," and in a two-volume collection published by the Supreme Court. In the selection of court judgments it has also been insured that both cases of rejection of petitions (*rafD*) and annulment of appeals court decisions (*naqD*) are represented, their numbers being 14 and 11, respectively. The reason for

TABLE 1. Topics Addressed in the Fatwas

Author	Topics
Qaradawi	Fixing wages; Islam and commerce; employment in banks; women's employment; graphic design work; fixing the price of goods by the state.
Ibn Baz	Buying bank shares; interest from banks; employment in banks; employment in restaurants.
Al-Moumni	Bribery; food imports; forbidden sales; bank loans; sale fraud; price markup.
Al-Ahmad	Profit margins; illegal incomes; down payments; late payment penalties; taxes; loan payments.
Fatwa Committee	Intermediaries; price markup; deferred payments.

TABLE 2. Topics Addressed in the Court Judgments

Source	Topics
Supreme Court Social Chamber	Employment contract; illicit competition; judicial fees; work injury; pensions; family benefits; power of attorney; administrative procedure; compensation for work accidents; employment termination; work-related car accidents.
Supreme Court Commerce Chamber	Auctions; debt declaration; judicial liquidation; abuse of authority; brokerage compensation; judicial guardianship; company director's responsibility; commercial rent; judicial liquidation and debts; bank–client relations; error in judgment dates; court officer's report; judicial liquidation and legal representation; tenant eviction.

selecting court judgments from Morocco is twofold. First, thanks to law studies in Morocco, the author of the present work is familiar with the Moroccan legal system and its context (curricula, journals, scholarship), and is thus able to provide an "insider" view of relevant issues (see discussion of characteristics of the Moroccan legal discourse community above). Second, compared with *'iftaa'*, which is more homogenous across the Arab world, since it is based on Quran and hadith, the legal systems are bound to vary a great deal because of sociopolitical and historical factors proper to each country. It is hoped, though, that other scholars from different Arab regions use their own "insider" perspectives to investigate legal discourse in their communities. The particular contextual elements of each community should lead to reliable and interesting insights about the rhetoric of legal texts. For example, in the present study the contact between French and Arabic in Morocco and characteristics of the Moroccan educational system are paramount in elucidating aspects of the court judgments considered. Complete references are given in Appendix A for fatwas and Appendix B for court judgments.

2.4. Analytical Procedure

The purpose of the study is to investigate rhetorical and linguistic features of court judgments and fatwas and to attempt to provide explanations for their occurrence in terms of contextual properties of each genre. In order to achieve this goal, the study adopts a qualitative analysis that seeks to provide a detailed description of the data, a clear presentation of the findings, and a rich interpretation of their significance. The analytical procedure consists in reading each court judgment and fatwa several times and identifying the recurrent rhetorical and linguistic patterns that support the purpose of each genre. The rhetorical analysis focuses on determining the moves utilized in each set of data, their order of occurrence, and their importance (obligatory or optional). As indicated earlier, the analysis draws upon Swales's seminal work on move analysis and the lexico-grammatical properties of genres (Swales 1990). In addition, the analysis of the court judgments uses insights from studies of the structure of legal decisions presented in Cornu (1990) for French and Bhatia (1993) for English as well as from studies I have conducted, using French and Arabic legal data (Fakhri 2002, 2009). In the case of fatwas, most available research focuses on their legal and cultural content, with only occasional statements about form that are far less elaborate than those made in the research on the structure of court judgments and thus only marginally useful from a linguistic perspective (Heyd 1969; Mallat 1996; Hallaq 2001). For example, Hallaq (2001:175), in his discussion of fatwas, made the following cursory observation about their form:

> Some jurists, such as Ibn Rushd, were in the habit of beginning their answer with the formula, "I have read your question and carefully considered it" . . . or some similar statement.

Other general descriptions of the form of fatwas are found in a study of Ottoman fatwas by Heyd (1969). The author notes, for example, that most of these fatwas begin with a pious invocation written in Arabic and that after the answer, some muftis add a postscript that gives further clarifications.

Regarding the relevant linguistic properties of the texts, the process of their identification is guided by research on the characteristics of written Arabic (Al-Batal 1990; Johnstone 1990, 1991; Fakhri 1998, 2004, 2005; see discussion above in chapter 1) and by legal discourse literature (Maley 1987; Bhatia 1992, 1993; Gibbons 1994; Feteris 1999; Fakhri 2002, 2008, 2009). Using as a point of reference linguistic features gleaned from these studies, the analysis focuses on those elements that serve to achieve particular discourse goals of the texts under consideration. These include complex syntactic patterns which are crucial for formulating elaborate legal arguments, formulaic language that allows for efficient writing, modes of citing secular legal sources (e.g., codes and statutes) that give the impression of a detached and objective intellectual style, and finally modes of citing *sharii'a* sources, mostly Quranic verses and hadith, which play an important role in enhancing the persuasive quality of fatwas.

The discussion of the findings benefits especially from genre analysis studies that attempt to account for the relationship between textual features and contextual factors (Swales 1990; Bhatia 1993; Duszak 1994; Fakhri 2009). The discussion also benefits from seminal work in discourse analysis and pragmatics such as that of Goffman (1981) and Grice (1991). It will be shown, for example, that digressions observed in fatwas are most aptly and insightfully accounted for in terms of Grice's maxim of relation and the factors that may motivate its violation or suspension (Grice 1991; Keenan 1976) and that Goffman's (1981) notion of "footing" can serve to elucidate muftis' shifts of social stance from jurists to counselors or teachers. The purpose of this eclectic approach is to provide a rich interpretation of the findings, evaluate their validity and significance with sufficient rigor, and relate them in a meaningful way to major themes and generalizations concerning language use.

The study also adopts a contrastive approach that considers similarities and differences between fatwas and court judgments. While at first sight this approach may raise questions about the comparability of the two sets of data, it has the advantage of enhancing the validity of interpretations put forward to account for some of the observed phenomena. For example, the contrasts help to detect the textual peculiarities of each set, which in turn facilitates the determination of the generic contextual factors that motivate them. The acceptability of the comparison can perhaps be better put in perspective by considering the following statement by the philosopher of science Abraham Kaplan (1963:266):

> No two things in the world are wholly alike, so that every analogy, however close, can be pushed too far; on the other hand no two things are wholly dissimilar, so that there is always an analogy to be drawn, if we choose to do so. The question to be considered in every case is whether or not there is something else to be learned from the analogy if we do choose to draw it.

The point made here is that, although fatwas and court judgments come from different contexts, they share quite a few properties. Both are intended to provide legal opinions; both deal with matters of law in that they are not concerned with establishing the facts of the cases presented to them but instead take these facts as correct;[12] and, as mentioned earlier, both sets of texts discuss similar topics, *muʿaamalaat,* that is, business-related issues. In other words, the types of texts are similar enough that comparing them is deemed quite legitimate, especially as such a comparison has the potential to yield important insights regarding relationships between textual features and their contexts of occurrence. For example, the comparison will show that both fatwas and court judgments support their opinions by referring to material from religious texts and legal codes, respectively. However, they differ with respect to the linguistic mechanisms for integrating the cited material into current texts, which facilitates the identification of the contextual factors proper to each genre that may explain these differences. Indeed, it will be argued that the observed textual differences are the result of the fact that fatwas and court judgments are intended for different audiences and that court judgments are legally enforceable whereas the fatwas are nonbinding. Furthermore, it will be shown in chapter 5 that comparisons between the fatwas and the court judgments regarding modes of argumentation are extremely beneficial for constructing a comprehensive model of Arabic legal argumentation that integrates in a coherent fashion ways of arguing from both genres. This is definitely something important to be learned from the analogy drawn between the two genres, to paraphrase Kaplan's terms.

The presentation of the analysis employs numerous excerpts from the Arabic texts considered with English translation. Since the focus is mostly on discourse phenomena, the Arabic transcription avoids minute morphophonological details that may make the presentation unnecessarily burdensome. The phonetic value of the letters in the transcription is similar to their English pronunciation except for the symbols given in Table 3. The translation is kept as close to the original as possible so as to maintain the flow of Arabic discourse but without obscuring meaning in the English version. Some readers may want to skip the transcription and rely only on the English translation. Readers interested in the Arabic details may read the Arabic transcription and even check Appendix E, where the excerpts are provided in the original Arabic script. Furthermore, since the discussion of the findings adopts various approaches to language study, an attempt is made to elucidate specialized theoretical constructs and other aspects of the linguistic models utilized to shed light on the data under consideration.

---

12. Assessing the accuracy of facts presented in lawsuits is the responsibility of lower courts rather than the Supreme Court. Muftis take for granted the facts presented to them by the questioner and base their responses on these facts.

TABLE 3. Phonetic Value of Symbols Used in the Arabic Transcription

dh	interdental voiced fricative (Arabic ذ)
th	interdental voiceless fricative (Arabic ث)
D	voiced pharyngealized dental stop (emphatic equivalent of [d], Arabic ض)
Dh	voiced pharyngealized interdental fricative (emphatic equivalent of dh, Arabic ظ)
T	voiceless pharyngealized dental stop (emphatic equivalent of [t], Arabic ط)
S	voiceless pharyngealized alveolar fricative (emphatic equivalent of [s], Arabic ص)
H	voiceless pharyngeal fricative (Arabic ح)
gh	voiced uvular fricative (Arabic غ)
q	voiceless uvular stop (Arabic ق)
x	voiceless uvular fricative (Arabic خ)
’	glottal stop (Arabic ء)
‘	voiced pharyngeal fricative (Arabic ع)

SUMMARY

This chapter has presented a concise discussion of the notion of genre, especially as viewed by the Swales model and its application in academic and professional settings. Particularly relevant aspects of the model are the relation between textual properties and properties of context, the notion of discourse community and its role in genre construction and maintenance, and move analysis as an important tool for identifying rhetorical patterns. The chapter has also described the institutional sources of the data and underscored some of the most important points that will be referred to later in the analysis of the data and the interpretation of the findings. These include the nonbinding nature of fatwas, the different bodies that issue them, and the traditional guidelines regarding their drafting. Also included are discussions of the characteristics of law professionals who regularly deal with court judgments, with particular emphasis on their French and Arabic educational background, their exposure to focused instruction in legal rhetoric, and their familiarity with Arabic–French bilingual documents and scholarly publications. Finally, the chapter describes the sample of texts selected and their topical content and outlines the analytical procedure adopted, highlighting its qualitative nature and its contrastive approach. The analysis relies on discussions of numerous excerpts from fatwas and court judgments and contrasts and compares these texts with respect to their most prominent linguistic and rhetorical features and the factors that motivate them.

Chapter Three
Rhetorical Analysis

The purpose of this chapter is to describe the rhetorical patterns found in court judgments (section 1) and fatwas (section 2) and to propose accounts of their occurrence in each genre. The description of the rhetorical patterns is based on a detailed analysis of the different moves used in the texts under consideration. A move is a portion of a text that is intended to accomplish a particular communicative function. Moves may be divided into submoves, may be obligatory or optional, often occur in a particular sequence, and may be recycled. As mentioned earlier, this type of move analysis is quite efficient in identifying important aspects of textual organizations, as clearly demonstrated in Swales's (1990) study of research article introductions and Bhatia's (1993) application of similar analysis in professional settings.

1. THE RHETORICAL STRUCTURE OF THE COURT JUDGMENTS

The court judgments considered for this study exhibit the following moves: Giving the History of the Case, Stating the Petitioner's Claims, Presenting the Opinion of the Court, and, finally, Pronouncing the Decision. These moves will be described and illustrated before discussing aspects of variation regarding their use.

1.1. Move 1: Giving the History of the Case

Since the Supreme Court focuses on the correct application of the law and is not concerned with establishing the facts of a case directly, its judgments rely on statements of facts presented in briefs and documents submitted by the parties and on earlier rulings by lower courts. Typically, this section begins with phrases such as (1) or (2).

(1) Haythu yustafaadu min wathaa'iqi almilaf wa min alqaraari alma-T'uuni fiih . . . 'anna . . .
Considering that it is deduced from the file documents and from the contested decision that . . .

(Al Milaf 2006, 9:310)

(2) Haythu yu'xadhu min 'anaaSiri almilaf wa min alqaraari al maT'uuni fiih . . . 'anna . . .
Considering that it is indicated from the components of the file and from the contested decision that . . .

(Supreme Court 2006, 66:175)

These introductory sentences are followed by a summary of the material facts, the legal actions taken by the parties, and the rulings of primary courts and courts of appeals. The section usually ends with the explicit statement that the petition seeks the annulment of the contested decision, as in (3).

(3) wa haadhaa huwa alqaraaru almaTluubu naqDuh min Tarafi al'ajiira.
And this is the decision that the employee seeks to get annulled.

(Supreme Court 2006, 64–65:362)

1.2. Move 2: Stating the Petitioner's Claims

This move presents the claims made by the petitioner, *aTTaalib,* regarding the validity of the contested decision and the points of law upon which these claims are based. The goal of petitioners is to seek the annulment and reversal of the decision rendered against them by a lower court. The move typically identifies the different grounds for annulment, *wasaa'ilu annaqD,* invoked by the petitioner, and states which aspect of the contested verdict is objected to, using verbs such as *'aaba, na'aa, 'aaxadha* "to blame," "to find fault with," or "to reproach," as in (4).

(4) fii sha'ni alfar'i al'awwal lilwasiilati al'uulaa Haythu tan'aa aTTaa'inatu 'alaa alqaraar xarqa alfaSlayn 452 . . . wa 345 . . . wa fasaada atta'liil . . .
Concerning the first branch of the first ground, where the petitioner faults the [lower court's] decision with violating articles 452 . . . and 345 . . . and with faulty justification . . .

(Supreme Court 2006, 64–65:240)

As shown in (4), petitioners often fault the lower court's decision with violating specific laws as well as with some general shortcoming such as bad justification or lack of legal basis. We should note that, although the main task of the court is to evaluate the legal merit of the petitioner's claims, the court occasionally considers defenses put forth by the respondent, as in (5).

(5) Haythu 'aThaara almaTluubu daf'an bi'adami qabuuli aTTalab li'anna aTTaaliba . . .
Considering that the respondent raised a defense seeking the rejection of the petition because the petitioner . . .
(Al Milaf 2005, 5:332)

The presentation of the claims ends with the clear indication of the petitioner's contention that the decision in question needs to be reversed (6).

(6) fa almaHakama bitamassukihaa bi'adami 'iHtiraami aTTaa'inati limuqtaDayaati alfaSl 12 takuunu qad 'allalat qaraarahaa ta'liilan xaaTi'an wa muxaalifan lilqaanuun mimmaa yu'arriDu alqaraara linnaqD.
The [lower] court, by holding that the petitioner did not heed the stipulations of article 12, has based its decision on faulty and unlawful justification, which exposes the decision to annulment.
(Supreme Court 2006, 66:337)

1.3. Move 3: Presenting the Opinion of the Court

In the description of this move we need to make a distinction between instances where the Supreme Court agrees with the petitioner's claims and those where it does not. In case of agreement, the Court, after discussing the petitioner's claims, indicates explicitly their validity, as in (7).

(7) Haythu thabatat SiHHatu maa na'aahu aTTaa'inu 'alaa alqaraar dhaalika 'anna . . .
Considering that what the petitioner faults the decision with is shown to be valid in that . . .
(Supreme Court 2006, 66:254)

The expression of agreement is supported by points of law and material facts and followed by the conclusion that the contested decision should be annulled, as in (8).

(8) dhaalika 'anna alfaSl 6 min Dhahiir 6/2/1963 ya'tabiru fii Hukmi Haadithati ashshughl alHaadithata aTTaari'ata lil'ajiir bayna makaani

assuknaa wa bayna makaani al'amal wa 'anna alqaraara almaT'uuna fiih lammaa qaDaa bixilaafi dhaalik yakuunu ghayra murtakizin 'alaa 'asaas . . . mimmaa yu'arriDuhu linnaqD.
Since article 6 of the decree of 2/6/1963 views as a work accident the accident that happens to the employee between his residence and his place of employment and since it has ruled differently, the contested judgment is not well grounded, which exposes it to annulment.
(Supreme Court 2006, 66:341)

We should note, however, that in many cases the agreement of the court with the petitioners' claims is implicit and no statements like (7) above are used.

In the case of disagreement with the petitioner, the Supreme Court's refutation of the latter's arguments is clearly signaled by the contrastive phrase *laakin Haythu 'anna* "However, considering that . . . ," which is then followed by the legal reasoning of the court. The court's arguments lead to the conclusion that the contested judgment is sound and that, consequently, the petitioner's request to invalidate it is unacceptable (9).

(9) . . . yakuunu alqaraaru ghayra xaariqin li'ayyi muqtaDaa wa mu'allalan bimaa fiihi alkifaaya wa alwasiilatu 'alaa ghayri 'asaas.
The [contested] judgment does not violate any legal stipulation and is sufficiently justified and the [petitioner's] argument is baseless.
(Supreme Court 2006, 64–65:231)

1.4. Move 4: Pronouncing the Decision

This move is very concise, and its language highly formulaic. Although its content is predictable in that it is the logical consequence of the argumentation in the previous moves, the inclusion of this move is crucial because, as a speech act, it solemnly declares the verdict of the court and conveys to the parties in a clear and unequivocal manner its illocutionary intent. The pronouncement of the decision is introduced by the phrase *lihaadhihi al'asbaab* "for these reasons" or, far less frequently, *li'ajlih* "because of this" followed by the formulaic expressions (10) or (11), depending on the outcome: rejection of the petitioner's request, *rafD*, or annulment of the lower court's decision, *naqD*.

(10) qaDaa almajlisu al'a'laa birafDi aTTalab . . .
The Supreme Court rules to reject the petition . . .

(11) qaDaa almajlisu al'a'laa binaqDi alqaraar . . .
The Supreme Court rules to annul the [lower court's] judgment . . .

The court may also include in its pronouncement stipulations concerning the responsibility for court costs payment and the remandment of the case to lower courts for further consideration.

The four moves described above capture the basic structure of the court judgments. However, in order to develop a more complete picture, the following additional remarks need to be made concerning structural variation among judgments. First, some court judgments (e.g., *Al Milaf* 2006, 9:309) begin by listing information about the date of the hearings, the identity of the litigants, the list of documents in the file, and about events of the proceedings such as calling the parties and listening to attorneys. Further discussion of this aspect is deemed to be of little value, since its import for the legal argumentation and the rhetoric used in the body of the texts is at best marginal. Second, Supreme Court chambers other than the ones considered for this study sometimes use peculiar features in their judgments. For example, judgments by the administrative chamber begin with a short introductory section about form before presenting the rest of the judgment dealing with the substance of case, as shown in (12).

(12) a. Introductory Section:
fii ashshakl
Haythu 'anna al'isti'naafa quddima daaxila al'ajal wa tamma wifqa ashshuruuTi alqaanuuniyya almutaTallaba liqabuulihi shaklan . . .
In form
Considering that the appeal was presented within the deadline and according to the legal conditions required for its formal acceptance . . .
b. Rest of the Judgment
fii aljawhar
Haythu yu'xadhu min wathaa'iqi almilaf . . .
In substance
Considering that it is deduced from the file documents . . .
(Supreme Court 2006, 64–65:313)

Third, the realization of the moves may vary. Move 1, giving the history of the case, does not always occupy a separate section; instead, details about the case are embedded as needed in the argumentation. This occurs particularly when there is an obvious factual or procedural element that is deemed sufficient for the courts to reach an immediate decision, as in the case of a petition that has named the wrong party in the lawsuit (*Al Milaf* 2005, 6:359). Moves 2 and 3 may be recycled, with the judgment describing separately each of the grounds presented by the petitioner

TABLE 4. Structure of a Court Judgment with Recycled Moves (Supreme Court 2006, 64–65:228)

History of the Case	Considering that it is indicated in the file documents and in the contested judgment rendered by the court of appeals . . . that the respondent presented a declaration of debt . . .
Petitioner's Claim 1	Regarding the first and the second grounds taken together, Considering that the petitioner faults the contested judgment with violating articles 687, 688, and 689 of the Code of Commerce . . .
Court's Opinion (refuting Claim 1)	However, considering that according to the stipulations of articles 686 and 687 of the Code of Commerce all debtors must send their debt declaration to the syndicate within a two-month deadline . . .
Petitioner's Claim 2	Regarding the third ground, . . . Considering that the petitioner faults the contested judgment with violating article 696 of the Code of Commerce . . .
Court's Opinion (refuting Claim 2)	However, considering that lawsuits brought within the framework of article 695 of the Code of Commerce . . .
Court's Decision	For these reasons, the Supreme Court rules to reject the petition and to hold the petitioner responsible for the court costs.

(Move 2) and then responding to it (Move 3). Table 4 gives the structure of a court judgment that illustrates the different moves and how they are recycled. The Arabic original is not given for ease of presentation.

2. THE RHETORICAL STRUCTURE OF THE FATWAS

Compared to the court judgments, the determination of the structure of the fatwas turns out to be more challenging because of important variations in their rhetorical patterns. Some fatwas provide concise and direct responses to the question posed by the questioner, *mustafti,* give supporting evidence, and may include additional material such as background information or advice. For example, in a fatwa concerning the permissibility of buying and selling bank shares, the mufti (a) answers directly that such activity is not permitted under *sharii'a* law, (b) provides evidence from the Quran and hadith, and (c) advises the questioner and Muslims in general to avoid all usurious transactions (Ibn Baz in Rifaa'ii 1988, 2:263–64). Other fatwas are more elaborate, couching their answers in theoretical discussions of topics in *sharii'a* law and providing historical accounts, anecdotes, and other background information. This is the case of the longest fatwa in the sample, a seven-page opinion about the validity of wage fixing by the state (Qaradawi 1981, 1:505–11). The mufti begins with a general discussion of the role of the state in *sharii'a* application and its obligation to insure justice and avoid conflict among members of the Muslim community, citing the Quran, hadith, and even a few anecdotes. Only at the end of this section does the mufti hint at the permissibility of wage fixing by the state, noting that *sharii'a* law guarantees fair wages for workers. This statement is supported by hadith and by lengthy quotes from an essay by the fourteenth-century mufti Ibn Taymiyya on *Hisba*, an institution designed to control merchandise quality and prices. The final section of the fatwa, subtitled *xulaaSa* "summary," restates, this time more directly, that *sharii'a* allows the state to intervene in wage fixing for the public good and to insure justice.

These preliminary observations are intended to give an idea about the degree of the rhetorical variation involved and highlight the challenge of abstracting general recurrent patterns from the texts considered. Thus while our concern here is to conduct a move analysis that best fits the data and captures regular patterns (section 2.1), it is equally important to devote sufficient discussion to rhetorical variation across the different fatwas (2.2) and to assess the adequacy of the analysis proposed (2.3).

2.1. Move Analysis of the Fatwas

The fatwas exhibit two obligatory moves: answering the question and providing evidence to support the answer. All the fatwas, except for one where the supporting evidence is uncertain, exhibit these two moves. This is quite predictable since the two moves reflect the main purpose of the fatwa as a communicative event: giving a convincing answer to the question posed by the *mustafti,* the fatwa seeker. In addition to the two obligatory moves, fatwas may include moves that provide different kinds of supplementary material with varying degrees of relevance. Since such additional moves are quite varied, and in order to avoid unnecessary fragmentation of the analysis and achieve an adequate level of generalization, these moves are grouped into two categories: those that are evaluative, involving for instance moral judgments on the part of the mufti, and that express speech acts such as advice, blame, or exhortation, and those that provide more information or explanation. For ease of presentation the first type will be referred to as "evaluative moves" and the second "informative moves." Let's consider the two obligatory moves first.

The questions addressed to the mufti typically concern whether a particular conduct or activity is permissible under *sharii'a* law. In the clearer cases, the answer is straightforward, either affirmative or negative, as in (13a) and (14a) respectively, followed by supporting evidence, (13b) and (14b).

TABLE 5. Structure of a Fatwa with Recycled Answer-Support Format

Answer (Q1)	It is permissible to sell a merchandise such as food or other kinds with deferred payment even for a higher price . . .
Support (Q1)	. . . because of the general application of God's saying: "[Quran]" . . . and because it was ascertained that the prophet [Honorific Expression] said: "[Hadith]"
Answer (Q2)	If a person buys a merchandise, he is not allowed to sell it in the same location . . . he must first obtain physical possession of the merchandise and transport it elsewhere. . . .
Support (Q2)	. . . Because of what was related by Ahmad [Honorific Expression] from Hakim Ibn Hizaam . . . "[Hadith]"

(13) a. Answering the Question (positive)
yajuuzu lil'insaani 'an yabii'a sil'atan 'ilaa 'ajalin ma'luum wa law zaada thamanu bay'ihaa 'ilaa 'ajal 'an qiimatihaa waqta bay'ihaa . . .
It is permissible to sell a merchandise with deferred payment even if the price charged exceeds its current value . . .

b. Providing Support
li'umuumi qawlihi ta'alaa: ". . ." wa limaa thabata 'ani annbiyyi Sallaa allaahu 'alayhi wa sallam 'annahu qaal: ". . ."
Because of the general application of God's saying: "Quran" and because it was ascertained that the prophet [honorific expression] said: "Hadith."

(The Committee in Shawadfi 1987:85)

(14) a. Answering the Question (negative)
laa yajuuzu bay'u 'ashumi albunuuki wa laa shiraa'uhaa . . .
It is not permissible to buy or sell bank shares . . .

b. Providing Support
li'annahaa mu'assasaatun rabwiyya laa yajuuzu atta'aawunu ma'ahaa liqawli allaahi subHaanah: ". . ." wa limaa thabata 'ani annabiyyi Sallaa allaahu 'alayhi wa sallam: ". . ."
Because they [the banks] are usurious institutions that should not be dealt with for God's [honorific expression] saying: "Quran" and because of what was ascertained about the prophet [honorific expression]: "Hadith."

(IbnBaz in Rifaa'ii 1988, 2:263)

The two moves illustrated above may be recycled in the same fatwa when, for example, the *mustafti* asks a two-part question. Table 5 gives the complete structure of the fatwa cited in (13) above, showing recycled answer-support organization. The fatwa deals with two related questions (Q1 and Q2): whether it is permissible to sell a merchandise at a higher price but with deferred payment and whether a merchandise can be resold in the same location where it was bought (The Committee in Shawadfi 1987:85).

Evaluative moves are mostly intended to give advice, but may also express blame or exhortation as shown in (15).

(15) Evaluative Moves

a. Advice

wa waSiyyatii laka wa lighayrika min almuslimiin huwa alHadharu min jamii'i almu'aamalaati arrabwiyya wa attaHdhiiru minhaa . . .
And my advice to you and to other Muslims is to be cautious and to warn about all usurious dealings . . .

(Ibn Baz in Rifaa'ii 1988, 2:263)

b. Exhortation

'innanii 'araa 'annahu min almuta'ayyin 'alaynaa 'an naxuuDa haad-hihi alma'raka al'i'laamiyya attiqniyya bikulli quwwa . . .
I believe that we should engage vehemently in this information technology battle . . .

(Qaradawi 2008:1)

c. Blame

laakin ma'a al'asafi ashshadiid almuslimuuna faqaduu aththiqata min ba'Dihim ba'Dan wa 'aSbaHat mu'aamalatu almuslimiina liba'Dihim ta'iishu fawDaa 'aarima.
But unfortunately Muslims have lost trust in each other and their dealings with each other have become marred by total disarray.

(Al-Moumni 1998:166)

It is worth noting that the language of evaluative moves more so than that of other moves exhibits features often seen as typical of Arabic prose: semantic couplets in (15a) (*alHadhar . . . wa attaHdhiir* "caution . . . and warning") and hyperbole and metaphor in (15b–c) (*alma'raka al'ilmiyya attiqniyya* "information technology battle," *bikulli quwwa* "with all force," *fawDaa 'aarima* "total disarray").

Informative moves tend to have a pedagogical function: they provide background information, definitions, and explanations as in (16).

(16) Informative Moves

a. Background Information

anniDhaamu al'iqtiSaadii fii al'islam yaquumu 'alaa 'asaasi muHa-arabati arribaa wa 'i'tibaarihi min kabaa'iri adhdhunuub . . .
The economic system in Islam is based on battling usury, which is considered a major sin . . .

(Qaradawi 1981, 1:529)

b. Definition

... yanhaa ʻan ʼistighlaali attaajir lilmushtarii aljaahili siʻra assilʻa wa haadhaa ashshaxSu yusammaa ʻinda alfuqahaaʼ: *almustarsil.*

[Islam] forbids a merchant to take advantage of the buyer who is unaware of the price of a merchandise. Such a buyer is referred to by jurists as *almustarsil* [unwitting buyer].

(Al-Ahmad 2003, 2:65)

c. Explanation

ʼinna ashsharriiʼa alʼislaamiyya taHruSu ʻalaa manʻi aDDarari wa aDDiraar ... wa qad jaaʼa fii alHadith: "laa Darara wa laa Diraar." ... wa qad rattaba alfuqhaaʼu ʼalaa haadhihi alqaaʻidati furuuʻan shattaa minhaa: ʼanna aDDarara yuzaal, wa ʼanna aDDarara laa yuzaalu bi aDDarar wa ʼanna aDDarara alxaaS yutaHammalu lidafʻi aDDarari alʻaam ...

Islamic law is devoted to the elimination of harm and prejudice ... the hadith says: "no harm and no prejudice." Jurists have divided this rule into several branches some of which are: a harm must be removed, but a harm must not be removed by another harm; and a private harm must be endured to protect against a public harm ...

(Qaradawi 1981, 1:506)

Example (16a) is taken from a section in the fatwa where the mufti, before answering a question about the permissibility of work in banks, discusses in general the gravity of usury in the Islamic economic system and, using hadith and verses from the Quran, recalls the duty of Muslims to resist it as an abhorrent sinful activity. In (16b), the technical term *mustarsil* "unwitting buyer" is defined, and in (16c) the mufti explains how jurists classify different legal ways of removing harmful situations from the community.

2.2. Variation in the Realization of Moves

In addition to fatwas with clear, concise answers and direct support from the Quran and the hadith, as illustrated above, other fatwas involve more nuanced answers and more elaborate methods of support given the indeterminacy or the complexity of the issues addressed. Regarding the answer to the question, the mufti may draw distinctions between different circumstances. Thus in his answer to a question about the imposition of monetary penalty for late debt payment, Al-Ahmad (2003:72) distinguishes between debtors who are solvent and those who are not and gives a different answer for each case.

Furthermore, the answer may need to be qualified, as in a fatwa about whether women are allowed to work outside the home. The mufti answers positively, but then proceeds to qualify his answer by enumerating several requirements that employed women must adhere to. This balancing act by the mufti is clearly apparent in (17), where the permissibility denoted by the verb *'ajaaz* "allow" is mitigated by the subsequent use of the noun *waajib* "obligation" and the adjective *muqayyad* "restrained."

(17) wa 'idhaa 'ajaznaa ʿamala almar'a faalwaajibu 'an yakuuna muqayyadan biʿiddati shuruuT . . .
Although we have allowed women's work outside the home, it must be restrained by several requirements . . .

(Qaradawi 1993, 2:303)

Finally, the answer may require consideration of different views given the lack of consensus. In this case, the mufti lays out the different positions on the issue at hand, and indicates the preponderant one (*alqawlu arraajiH*). Thus in a fatwa about the legality of earnest money in sales, the mufti states that some *fuqahaa'* "religious scholars" allow it, while others do not, and then draws the following conclusion:

(18) wa alqawlu biSiHHati bayʿi alʿurbuun huwa 'arjaHu alqawlayni fii almas'ala limaa fii dhaalika min taHqiiqi maSaaliHi alʿibaad wa xaaSSatan 'annahu lam yathbut annahyu ʿan bayʿi alʿurbuuni ʿan arrasuul [honorific expression].
Regarding the two views on this issue, the view that earnest money is legal is the preponderant one because it promotes public good and in particular because it was not ascertained that the prophet had prohibited it.

(Al-Ahmad 2003:71)

What is interesting about this fatwa is that the mufti initially cites a hadith that explicitly prohibits the practice of earnest money, but then dismisses it as *Daʿiif* "weak." A weak hadith is one whose veracity is doubtful, for example because the integrity of the *'isnaad,* the chain of transmission of the hadith, has been somehow compromised. Instead, the mufti uses the absence of any other hadith on this issue to support his position. Sometimes the mufti lists the various opinions about a particular issue without taking a position himself, as in a fatwa about the price markup ratio allowed by *sharii'a.* The mufti simply states that some scholars limit that ratio to one sixth of the cost, others to one third, while a third group claims that there are no restrictions (Al-Moumni 1998:171).

There is also a great deal of variation regarding the ways the answer is supported. While the most straightforward way for the mufti to support his opinion is through reference to the Quran and the hadith as earlier examples show, muftis sometimes have to resort to other methods of support, especially when difficult or controversial issues are considered. Three such methods are briefly discussed here to illustrate the variety of means available to muftis: reference to previous fatwas, argument by analogy, and application of a general legal principle.[1] It is worth noting that these methods are quite similar to those found in secular legal opinions as shown, for example, in the Feteris (1999:7) review of theories of judicial argumentation in Western legal traditions.

Regarding reference to precedent, the mufti may introduce the opinion of other muftis, a favorite one being the prolific fourteenth-century mufti Ibn Taymiyya. In the fatwa regarding wage fixing by the state discussed earlier, the mufti refers extensively to Ibn Taymiyya's position that *waliyyu al'amr* "the head of state" not only *may* intervene to fix wages equitably, but *has the obligation* to do so if, for example, a small group of craftsmen with special skills try to take advantage of the community by requiring unreasonably high compensation for their services (Qaradawi 1981:505). Reasoning by analogy extends the application of "a rule" used to resolve a particular issue to a new but presumably similar issue. As part of an argument against employment in usurious banks, Qaradawi (1981:529) draws a comparison between alcohol consumption and the practice of usury, referring to a hadith that prohibits not only consuming alcohol but also preparing and serving it (19).

(19) la'ana allaahu alxamra wa shaaribahaa wa saaqiihaa wa 'aaSirahaa . . .
God curses alcohol and the person who drinks it, serves it, or prepares it . . .

A similar reasoning is adopted in order to forbid working for usurious banks even in cases where one's own job in such institutions does not involve dealing directly with interest-based transactions. The similarity between the two situations, according to the fatwa, lies in the fact that they are both instances of *atta'aawunu 'alaa al'ithmi wa al'udwaan*

1. Another way for muftis to support their opinion, which is not exemplified in the fatwas considered, is to resort to linguistic analysis to interpret a particular text. One such case concerns the validity of praying alone behind the rows in a mosque, which hinges on the interpretation of the hadith *laa Salaata limunfaridin xalfa aSSaf* "no prayer for someone who prays alone behind the rows." The issue, according to the mufti, is how to interpret the negation in the sentence. Is the negation in the phrase *laa Salaata* "no prayer" "a negation of validity" (*nafyu aSSiHHa*) or "a negation of perfection" (*nafyu alkamaal*)? If it is the first case, then the prayer is not valid; if it is the second, then the prayer is valid, but not perfect. In other words, praying within the rows is preferred (Ibn Uthaymiin, n.d.: 88).

"collaboration on sin and transgression," a sort of complicity theory (see further discussion of this principle in chapter 4, section 2).

The mufti may also apply general principles often as a means of reconciling *sharii'a* precepts with the realities and the concerns of contemporary Muslim communities. This can be illustrated by two fatwas which give opposing answers to the question regarding employment in banks that engage in usurious interest-based transactions. One fatwa expresses the view that such employment is not permissible because the Quran and the hadith explicitly prohibit any involvement, direct or indirect, in usurious activities (Ibn Baz in Rifaa'ii 1988, 2:280). The other fatwa, while acknowledging such prohibition, proceeds to argue, and quite cogently, that the prohibited activities are so widespread in "our economic system and financial institutions" that the situation cannot be changed or otherwise influenced in any meaningful way by an individual's refusal to join the banking profession. Given this state of affairs, the mufti declares that bank employment is permissible, invoking the general principle of *aDDaruura* "necessity" that is often utilized to assuage potentially severe consequences of the automatic application of *sharii'a* law (Qaradawi 1981:529).[2] This principle is also cited elsewhere to permit international money transfer (Al-Moumni 1998:166) and to allow the state to determine the price of goods and merchandise (Qaradawi 2008). Sometimes it is the nonapplicability of the principle that is invoked: Sheikh Ibn Baz (Riffaa'ii 1988, 3:351), for example, discards necessity as a basis for permitting work in institutions that serve alcohol or pork, arguing that one should be able to find employment in other economic sectors that do not violate *sharii'a* law.

In sum, the fatwas exhibit a great deal of variation with respect to the types of moves they include (the obligatory moves of "answering the question" and "providing support" plus any number of evaluative and informative ones) and with respect to the amount of elaboration involved in the realization of these moves, which often depends on the complexity and/or the controversial nature of the issues considered.

2.3. Assessing the Analysis

The analysis presented above attempts to identify recurrent rhetorical moves in the fatwas and at the same time notes variation in the realization of these moves. However, the degree of variation observed raises the

2. The principle of *aDDaruura* "necessity" is based on quranic verses such as *yuriidu allaahu bikum alyusra wa laa yuriidu bikum al'usr* "Allah wants ease for you and does not want hardship for you."

question whether the most basic fatwas with a simple answer-support format, on the one hand, and, on the other hand, the most extended ones that include elaborate discussions and a significant amount of tangential material, should still be considered as belonging to the same genre. There are two possible ways of thinking about this issue. The first one is to view this variation on a complexification continuum where different fatwas can be placed according to the degree of elaboration of their answer and support and the amount of supplementary material added. The following is an approximation of such a continuum: Simple answer-support format (e.g., unambiguous answer with support from the Quran) > simple answer-support with limited supplementary material (e.g., advice) > elaborate answer-support (e.g., considering different possible answers and using precedent or analogy) with limited supplementary material > elaborate answer-support with extended supplementary material (e.g., explanations, illustrations, advice, anecdotes). The obvious advantage of this continuum view is that it accommodates the *'iftaa'* discourse community labeling of all these texts as fatwas, as indicated in the titles of the various collections. The continuum view is also consistent with Carolyn Miller's (1984:151) contention that "a rhetorically sound definition of genre must be centered not on the substance or the form of discourse but on the action it is used to accomplish." In other words, regardless of formal differences, the fatwas accomplish the same social action, namely providing believers with knowledge about *sharii'a* that will help them lead lives consistent with its precepts.

The second option is to view the most extended fatwas as qualitatively different from those with focused answer-support and an occasional item of advice, definition, or anecdote, for example. Such a dichotomous approach skirts the problem of "forcing" on the most extended fatwas the move analysis outlined above. Thus the structure of Qaradawi's (1981, 1:505–11) lengthy fatwa on wage fixing by the state, for example, may now be viewed as qualitatively different from other, more basic fatwas. As mentioned earlier, the fatwa begins with an extensive discussion of the role of the state in general before addressing in a very elaborate and erudite fashion the specific question posed by the *mustafti*, the fatwa seeker. This structure is reminiscent of essays with general-to-specific or "funnel"-type organization, and the preliminary section of the fatwa is amenable in its own right to a move analysis similar to Swales's (1990) analysis of research article introductions. Furthermore, the separation of extended fatwas from the rest finds support in old taxonomies of Arabic legal discourse in that these fatwas are very similar to what has traditionally been known as *risaala,* a type of legal essay. Hallaq (2001:169) describes this genre in the following terms:

> It was the custom that only the most distinguished *muftis,* when faced with a problem of frequent occurrence or of fundamental importance, would rise to the occasion by writing a *risaala* in which lengthy and complex arguments were constructed.

Whichever interpretation of the structural variation of the fatwas is adopted, it is clear that the fatwas exhibit a far higher degree of variation than the court judgments. The two sets of data are also different with respect to the degree of relevance of the content of their respective moves; while the content of the court judgment is to the point, some fatwa moves clearly constitute digressions that go beyond simply answering the question and providing support for the answer. The discussion that follows elaborates on these two main differences.

3. DISCUSSION

3.1. Degree of Structural Variation

The main task here is to consider contextual factors related to each genre (the fatwas and court judgments) that may account for the observed differences between them regarding structural variation. I will discuss the structural regularity in the court judgments first before turning to the extensive variation in the fatwas. The regular patterns found in the court judgments can best be accounted for through borrowing from French. As shown in Fakhri (2002), Moroccan court judgments have been influenced by the French model and have borrowed a well-established ready-made structure that easily accommodates content drawn from local secular laws, which are themselves compiled according to Western traditions in the form of codes and statutes with numbered divisions and subdivisions. The study provides evidence for this rhetorical borrowing by comparing three types of data: (a) traditional Moroccan judgments by a judge with typical Islamic education consisting essentially of quranic studies and Islamic law and theology,[3] (b) French court judgments obtained from law manuals such as Mendegris and Vermelle (1996) and Sériaux (1997), and (c) secular judgments rendered by modern Moroccan courts. The comparison clearly shows great similarity between the French judgments and the secular Moroccan ones. Both exhibit an argumentative

3. The traditional Moroccan judgments were rendered by Al Hassan Ben Al Haj Mohamed Laamaarti, a well-known *qaaDi* "Islamic judge" who served in the 1940s and 1950s in Chefchawen, Morocco. The judgments, 123 in total, have been compiled in a collection edited by Abdelali Alabboudi (1986), a former justice in the Moroccan Supreme Court.

structure consisting of a number of premises leading to the statement of the verdict. The traditional Moroccan judgments, on the other hand, show a narrative-like structure with, first, an identification of plaintiffs, defendants, and solicitors and a description of the material facts of the case, followed by a recounting of the interaction between the parties and the judge. The final section describes in a series of chronologically ordered clauses the judge's decision-making process (see Fakhri 2002 for further details). The similarity between the French judgments and the secular Moroccan ones is further manifested in the use of the same phrases, which cannot be attributed to coincidence. Examples of such phrase are *attendu que . . .* , *Haythu 'anna . . .* "Considering that . . . ," *sur le premier et deuxième moyens réunis . . .* , *fii sha'ni alwasiilati al'uulaa wa aththaaniya mujtami'atayn . . .* "concerning the first and second grounds taken together," and *pour ces raisons . . . lihaadhihi al'asbaab . . .* "for these reasons . . ." Given these important similarities in structure and the equivalence of many phrases, any claim that these patterns have developed independently in each language will be untenable, especially considering the overwhelming circumstantial evidence based on the long contact between the two languages during the French protectorate in Morocco in the first half of the twentieth century. Since that time Moroccan law faculties have adopted French curricula with focused instruction in legal argumentation and rhetoric as discussed earlier (see chapter 2, section 2).[4] It is also obvious that borrowing has occurred from French to Arabic and not the other way around. Thus while one may agree with Hatim's (1997:166) assertion that ". . . [Arabic texts] are no less logical (i.e., proof-oriented) than texts which explicitly observe time-honored Aristotelian models of logic" or even concede that particular Arabic texts may exhibit some form of syllogistic organization, the highly precise equivalence of patterns found in French and Arabic court judgments and the sociolinguistic circumstances mentioned above preclude any explanation other than borrowing.

Although they did not specifically use a move analysis approach, Cornu (1990) and Fakhri (2002) provide a discussion of the structure of French court judgments that can easily be recast in terms of moves.

4. The borrowing of patterns from French legal discourse is also manifested in other genres, such as research articles. Fakhri (2009) has documented such borrowing by examining an important similarity between law articles by French authors and Arabic articles by Moroccan legal scholars: both tend to adopt a two-part structure in organizing the content of their articles. Mendegris and Vermelle (1996:124) emphasize the necessity of this binary structure and describe it as a *moule particulièrement rigoureux* "a particularly rigorous mold" justified by the adversarial nature of the justice system, where opposing interests tend to be "organized around two poles."

Cornu (1990:338) views the court judgment as a response of the judge to the request of the parties: "Un jugement est la réponse du juge à la demande des parties." Consequently, he proposes the following general structure of court judgments, allowing for variation resulting from the type of jurisdiction considered:

1. The question
   A. Summary of the case circumstances
   B. Consideration of the parties' request
2. The answer
   A. Justification
   B. Solution

Cornu's analysis reflects the traditional binary division preferred in French legal discourse (Mendegris and Vermelle 1996:124): the judgment includes two main components, and in turn each of these has two subcomponents. However, with some adjustment, this pattern can be matched with the move analysis of court judgments presented earlier. Such matching is also possible in the case of the Fakhri study (2002:161), which points out in particular the similarity between French and Moroccan judgments regarding their overall organization. It is worth noting that the structure of English legal cases discussed in Bhatia (1993) is quite similar to the patterns outlined here for French (and their reflexes in Arabic), which seems to underscore a degree of homogeneity in Western legal rhetoric. This is especially true of Bhatia's (1993:135–36) Move 3, Arguing the Case, with its submoves (stating the history of the case, presenting arguments, deriving *ratio decidendi*) and Move 4, Pronouncing the Judgment.

In sum, the high regularity of the structural patterns in the court judgments of the present study reflects the French model and is maintained thanks to repeated practice by the Moroccan discourse community of judges, lawyers, and other law professionals who over time have got used to it and perhaps even appreciated it as an efficient mode of communication that allows them to devote their attention to the complexities of legal content rather than worry about form and textual organization. Furthermore, the maintenance of the structure of court judgments is favored by the type of interaction between the parties concerned with their production and use. The patterns found in these texts reflect not only judges' rhetorical choices but also the petitioners', since judges, when drafting their opinions, have to take into consideration the kind of arguments put forward by the petitioners, the way these are fleshed out, and even the sequence in which they are made. In a sense the shape of the judgment results from joint contributions by different participants with divergent agendas and high stakes in the resolution of the issue at hand. The effect of such constraints is to preclude or at least render difficult and less likely any innovation or departure from customary patterns exhibited in the court judgments.

Now let's consider the extensive structural variation found in the fatwas. Compared with court judgments, the fatwas are far less constrained, and their extensive variation reflects the diversity of participants' characteristics and the variable complexity of the topics addressed. Regarding participants, any member of the Muslim community, from private individuals and socioeconomic institutions to government entities (see Haddad 1996 and Messick 1996 for examples), may address a query to any mufti, be it a simple local imam such as Al-Moumni (1998), a renowned religious scholar such as Sheikh Qaradawi (1981), or an official institution in charge of *'iftaa'* (see footnote 3 in chapter 2). In contrast to the case of court judgments, where participants (e.g., judges and lawyers) can be assumed to have equal standing regarding knowledge of legal matters, muftis are privileged participants in that they are perceived by *mustaftis* to be the possessors of knowledge about *sharii'a* law and, therefore, have more latitude in the formulation of their fatwas. Differences in the scholarly preparation of muftis also add to variation in fatwa patterns in that erudite self-confident muftis are more likely to engage in elaborate innovative discussions and extensive sermonizing. Muftis with more modest scholarly backgrounds are more prone to simply convey information obtained from *sharii'a* texts, including other fatwas.[5]

As indicated by examination of fatwa collections and their tables of contents, the topics covered are extremely varied and range from personal conduct, social relations and customs, and religious rituals to family relations, inheritance, and business transactions. Even within the same topic category such as the last one, which has been selected for the present study, one finds a great diversity of subtopics (e.g., banking interest, sale fraud, profit margins, and employment issues). This wide range of topics addressed by fatwas gives rise to diversity of opinion, which in turn leads to a great deal of variation in how the fatwas are constructed. The more concise fatwas with simple answer-support format are typically those that deal with questions that have been settled and for which there are explicit answers in the Quran and hadith. On the other hand,

5. Differences between muftis regarding their scholarly credentials are captured by the traditional ranking of muftis. A *mustaqill* "independent" is a mufti who uses various methods of reasoning and may provide an "independent" opinion, whereas a *muqallid* "imitator" is a mufti who gives the dominant opinion in a particular *madhhab*, or school of thought (see discussion in chapter 2).

questions that do not have straightforward answers in religious texts and for which there is lack of consensus provide preeminent muftis with a great deal of latitude and with an opportunity to construct extended fatwas with sophisticated argumentation and means of support. This is the case of fatwas dealing with modern-day issues such as work in graphic design or questions about overarching issues such as the role of the state in regulating wages (Qaradawi 2008, 1981).

3.2. Difference in Degree of Relevance

A major difference between court judgments and fatwas concerns the relevance of their content. As shown above, the fatwas often go beyond responding to the question posed and include additional information, advice, blame, and exhortation. These additions are unsolicited and clearly not germane to answering questions about the position of *sharii'a* on the issues at hand. In (15b) above, the mufti does not limit himself to stating the position of *sharii'a* regarding graphic design, but instead proceeds to exhort the Muslim community "to engage vehemently in [this] information technology battle." Similarly, in (15c) the mufti's lamentations about the claim that nowadays Muslims do not trust each other have little relation to the question of the legality of bank loans. These digressions are all the more unexpected given that traditional treatises on mufti conduct (see discussion of *'adab almufti* in chapter 2, section 2.1) explicitly require that muftis' answers be concise and free from speculations. In contrast to fatwas, the court judgments avoid such digressions and keep their discussions to the point. In fact, the court often opts not to unnecessarily examine all the arguments presented by the parties for it to reach a verdict when the consideration of a single plea is deemed sufficient for it to reach a decision, as indicated in (20).

(20) wa biSarfi annaDhar 'an baHthi baaqii al'awjuh wa alwasiilati al'uxraa . . . qaDaa almajlisu al'a'laa binaqDi wa 'ibTaali alqaraari alma-T'uuni fiih . . .
And without considering the remaining aspects or the other plea . . . the Supreme Court rules to annul and invalidate the contested judgment . . .

(Supreme Court 2006, 66:341)

The question that needs to be addressed, then, is how to account for the observed digressions in the fatwas. One of the most insightful approaches to understanding the issue of relevance in language use is Grice's (1991) view that social interaction is based on cooperation among participants who adhere to a number of conversational rules. I propose therefore to frame the discussion of digressions in fatwas in terms of this Gricean approach.[6] This will allow us to account for these digressions in a meaningful way, since they are considered within the general issue of relevance rather than treated as a peculiar phenomenon. Grice suggests that successful social interaction is guided by what he terms the "cooperative principle" and identifies conversational rules or maxims that must be adhered to. One of these is the maxim of relation that requires interlocutors to make their contribution relevant to the topic of the conversation.[7] For example, if a speaker asks a question, the hearer is expected to respond in a relevant manner. The nonobservance of the maxim can vary in terms of its magnitude, as in (21), which illustrates different degrees of relevance of the responses to the question "can you tell me what time it is?"

(21) a. Question: Can you tell me what time it is?
Answer: It's eight o'clock.
b. Question: Can you tell me what time it is?
Answer: "Countdown" just started.
c. Question: Can you tell me what time it is?
Answer: It's eight o'clock. I think you should go home. This park is not safe at night.
d. Question: Can you tell me what time it is?
Answer: Times are changing!

In (21a) the response is clearly relevant and in (21d) clearly irrelevant, the respondent being totally uncooperative. But participants may flout the maxim of relation without being uncooperative, as in (21b), where the respondent simply forces the questioner to make an effort to draw the correct inference from the seemingly inappropriate response. Both participants are assumed to know the time when the television show

6. Grice's Cooperative Principle has been used in several disciplines, including philosophy and linguistics, which has resulted in different interpretations of the term *cooperation* (Lindblom 2001; Davies 2007). It is beyond the scope of the present discussion to address this theoretical issue. The usual meaning of the term *cooperation* adopted in linguistic studies is plausible and intuitively appealing and has been used with much success in understanding interaction in various social and professional contexts.

7. The other maxims proposed by Grice are the following:

The maxim of quality: "Be truthful"
The maxim of quantity: "Be informative"
The maxim of manner: "Be clear"

Grice's maxims have been widely used to shed light on social interaction in various settings, including, for example, courtroom discourse (Penman 1987).

"Countdown" begins, and on the basis of this knowledge the questioner should be able to make sense of the response. In (21c) the first portion of the response, "it's eight o'clock," is relevant; however, the speaker goes on to give advice and justification. This type of interaction is plausible for instance when the questioner is a young person asking a police officer about the time. In this case the apparent violation of the maxim of relation can be quite telling in that it implies a particular power relation between interlocutors: an authority figure addressing an "imprudent" youth.

It is suggested here that the case of fatwas is similar to the hypothetical circumstances illustrated in (21c). The maxim of relation is not violated but simply suspended because of relevant properties of fatwa issuing as a communicative event. This is in line with Keenan's (1976) study of speech communities in Madagascar, which was intended to test the cross-cultural applicability of Grice's maxim of quantity that requires speakers to be as informative as necessary, not more, not less. The author found that under certain circumstances the maxim is suspended and there is no expectation that interlocutors adhere to it. Keenan (1976:78) states that "whether a Malagasy conforms to the maxim 'Be informative' or not depends on certain socially relevant features of the interactional setting." Such features include the significance of the information sought, interpersonal relations, and even the gender of the speakers. Commenting on this finding, Thomas (2001:120) suggests that "suspensions of the maxims may be culture-specific." The point here is that a similar account can be extended to the present case: the maxim of relation is suspended, enabling muftis to go beyond answering the question posed to them and to add explanations and engage in advising and exhortation. The suspension of the maxim of relation and the digressions to which it leads are facilitated by the fact that muftis tend to commend a great deal of respect, deference, and even obsequiousness on the part of fatwa seekers, who look up to them presumably because of their knowledge of *sharii'a* law, their piety, and their rectitude.

Furthermore, the diverse competencies of muftis make it easy for them to add other moves besides answering the question and supporting their answer. Many muftis, especially distinguished ones, often occupy different functions in the community: in addition to being muftis, they may also hold positions as teachers and preachers in mosques.[8] The various moves identified represent the mufti's shifts in footing, a notion

8. The authors of the fatwas considered in this study have occupied positions as imams (preachers) and teachers of Islamic studies and *sharii'a* law. Before his appointment as Grand Mufti of Saudi Arabia, Sheikh Abdulaziz Ibn Baz served as a judge, as a professor at Riyad Religious Institute, and as chancellor of the Islamic University in Madina. Sheikh

developed by Goffman (1981) to capture the changes in social capacities that allow interlocutors to project different selves at different points of the interaction. Thus, when drafting fatwas, the mufti assumes different roles. As a mufti proper, he answers the question and provides support for his opinion; when he discusses and explains additional issues or gives definitions of terms, he clearly assumes the role of a teacher; and finally, when he volunteers advice and guidance, his footing is that of a moral counselor. In other words, the structure of fatwas seems to reflect muftis' different rhetorical personae, as it were, and juxtaposes their multifaceted rhetorical expertise gained through their functions as muftis, teachers, and preachers. This is clearly indicated by changes in the language of fatwas, which is consistent with Goffman's (1981:128) suggestion that shifts in footing are often "language-linked." The footing is sometimes overtly stated, as in the following example where, before answering the question addressed to him, the mufti assumes the role of teacher by explicitly indicating his intention to draw attention to an important fact in *sharii'a* law that many people may be ignorant of. This stretch of discourse highlights inequality of status between lay fatwa seekers and a mufti who possesses an important body of knowledge, *sharii'a* law, that he deems necessary to transmit to the "many" people who lack such knowledge.

(22) 'awaddu 'an 'unabbiha hunaa 'alaa Haqiiqatin shar'iyyatin muhimmatin qad yaghfalu 'anhaa kathiirun mina annaasi 'aw yajhaluunahaa . . .
I would like to draw attention here to an important fact in *sharii'a* that many people do not heed or are ignorant of . . .

(Qaradawi 1981, 1:505)

When the mufti assumes the role of moral counselor, the language used often reflects a personal tone whereby the mufti addresses the questioner directly. Previously mentioned expressions such as *'innanii 'araa 'annahu mina almuta'ayyin 'alaynaa 'an . . .* "I believe that we should . . ." and *wa waSiyyatii laka . . .* "and my advice to you . . ." (see examples 15 and 16 above) abound with references to self and to addressees (e.g.,"I," "we," "you") and suggest a sense of familiarity and involvement that is absent, for example, in the more detached explanations of trade laws provided by the writer as a mufti proper. We will discuss later in chapter 4 how syntactic complexity of the discourse of fatwas also varies with each footing.

Yusuf Qaradawi served as dean of *Sharii'a* faculty in Qatar. Al-Ahmad preached in mosques and lectured on Islamic studies in Syria and United Arab Emirates (Al-Ahmad 2003:6–7), while Al-Moumni was imam in Badr Mosque in Oujda, Morocco, and lectured at Nasr Mosque in Rotterdam, The Netherlands (Al-Moumni 1998:7–9).

Finally, the addition of seemingly unnecessary material may potentially serve to enhance the persuasive quality of the fatwa. Given the nonbinding character of fatwas, providing advice and erudite explanations makes the mufti appear to be a very knowledgeable and caring person, which creates a favorable impression on his audience and makes his opinion more convincing. Additional material may also serve as a rhetorical softener that facilitates the acceptance of fatwas, especially those that deal with controversial issues. This is the case of the fatwa mentioned earlier where the mufti asserts that it is permissible for women to seek employment outside the home. Having thus stated the position of *sharii'a* on the issue, the mufti proceeds to add warnings and numerous conditions and constraints regarding the type of jobs women may hold and details the manner in which they should behave in public. At first sight, these additions may seem unwarranted and may discourage women from exercising their right to employment for fear of infringing upon expected mores. However, they constitute useful rhetorical strategies for enhancing the acceptability of the mufti's position in view of the fact that there are more conservative opinions that argue that women should stay at home and take care of their families.[9] In other words, from the perspective of a conservative audience, the addition of constraints makes the fatwa more palatable. For a more "liberal" audience, acknowledging rights with constraints, though not optimal, can be perceived as a better alternative to denying them altogether.[10] In sum, the observed digressions are motivated by characteristics of muftis and their relation to fatwa seekers. Although they may be questionable for some, they do not seem to undermine the popularity of fatwas as suggested by the widespread solicitation of muftis and the proliferation of fatwas in various media, including print media, radio and television, and the Internet (Messick 1996; Farquhar 2009; see also discussion in chapter 2, section 2.1). They

9. In its December 3, 2008, online issue, the Moroccan newspaper *Aujourd'hui le Maroc* (http://www.aujourdhui.ma) reported on a fatwa that denies women's work outside the home, especially if the husband objects to it, and considers that a woman's main mission is to care for her family and "*préparer les hommes et les femmes du futur*" (prepare future men and women). However, the report questioned the qualifications of the writer of the fatwa, since his title was a "*chercheur dans les sciences de la charia*" (a researcher in the sciences of *sharii'a*) and not a genuine mufti.

10. Fatwas that deal with social and family issues are particularly revealing with respect to the addition of statements apparently intended to mitigate opinions that may be controversial or unacceptable to segments of the community. For example, in a fatwa about the possibility of including in a marriage contract divorce stipulations favorable to women, the mufti answers that "religion [Islam] does not forbid a woman to stipulate in her marriage contract provisions allowing her to divorce herself from her husband." But then he adds the following:

seem to be tolerated and, in the case of additions intended to advise and exhort, perhaps even appreciated, although they are not explicitly sought.

Digressions, additions, and shifts in footing and their concomitant suspension of the maxim of relation are absent in the court judgments, where the judges render a legally enforceable decision that seeks the application of the rule of law in an objective and detached manner. The content of the judgments is focused and to the point, and devoid of unnecessary evaluative commentary and rhetorical manipulations. However, one might argue that the first move in the court judgments, giving the history of the case, seems to flout Grice's maxim of quantity (see footnote 7 above), since such history is known to the litigants and their attorneys and, thus, may be deemed uninformative and superfluous. This apparent violation may be mitigated and accounted for in two ways. First, while the history of the case is known to the parties concerned, the latter need to be reassured that the court has considered the documents presented to it, is aware of their factual and legal content, and has based its decision on that content. Sometimes the court seeks to strike a balance between the need for concision, a valued quality in legal argumentation, and its readiness to accommodate the litigants' expectations that adequate consideration has been given to their contentions. Thus, without relating the detailed content of a document presented to it, the court may simply point out that it has considered it, as in (23).

(23) binaa'an 'alaa al'awraaqi al'uxraa almudlaa bihaa fii almilaf . . .
On the basis of the other documents presented in the file . . .
(*Al Milaf* 2005, 6:354)

Second, because Supreme Court judgments are intended to set precedent, the history of the case is crucial for lower court judges and other law professionals, since it enables them to understand the rationale behind the decision and to compare and contrast the current case with future ones they will have to deal with.

And here we must advise our young sisters not to be self-conceited and abuse this right. . . . We must also keep in mind that such divorce stipulations may not be acceptable to honorable husbands, even though they are not legally prohibited. (Al-Ahmad 2003, 2:108).

This example shows how the mufti goes beyond simply stating what, according to him, the *sharii'a* position is; he proceeds to soften his opinion by advising "our young sisters" and warning them not to offend "honorable husbands." Perhaps a more "progressive" mufti would instead address his advice to reluctant husbands so that they respect this contractual right given to women by *sharii'a*, thus showing their adherence to Islamic precepts, even though they may not be advantageous to them.

SUMMARY

This chapter has presented an analysis of the rhetorical patterns in court judgments and fatwas in terms of the moves used to achieve their purposes. It has been found that the court judgments exhibit four moves: giving the history of the case, stating the petitioner's claims, presenting the opinion of the court, and pronouncing the decision. The most important variation regarding the realization of these moves is that, due to the complexity of the petitioner's argumentation, Move 2 (stating the petitioner's claims) and Move 3 (presenting the opinion of the court) may be recycled in order to accommodate the various steps of the argument. The analysis of the fatwas has turned out to be more challenging because of the diversity in their textual organization. It has been possible, however, to identify two obligatory moves: answering the question and providing support for the opinion given. In addition to these two basic moves, fatwas may add any number of evaluative moves, such as advice, or informative moves, such as explanation. It has been argued that this complexity of fatwa organization can be viewed along a complexification continuum or in terms of subcategories of fatwas such as basic fatwas, extended fatwas, and *risaala,* an elaborate essay on a complex issue in *sharii'a* law.

The regularity of the rhetorical patterns in the court judgments is attributed to the fact that these patterns have been borrowed as a whole from French judicial discourse and maintained in Arabic because of their efficiency and repeated utilization as a readymade argumentative structure that allows judges to concentrate on the content of arguments rather than form. The greater variation of the rhetoric of fatwas is accounted for by referring to contextual factors related to the use of fatwas, such as the topics addressed, the nonbinding nature of fatwas, and the rhetorical expertise of muftis. Muftis may simply be asked about issues that have been unambiguously settled in *sharii'a* law or, on the contrary, may have to deal with controversial topics that require elaborate argumentation. It has also been argued that the digressions that often occur in fatwas are motivated by the enhancement of the persuasive quality of the fatwa and the mufti's desire to make his opinion acceptable to skeptical or reluctant audiences. The digressions are also facilitated by the fact that muftis possess varied rhetorical expertise gained through different positions they often occupy in their communities (e.g., as muftis, teachers, and imams).

Chapter Four
Linguistic Properties of Court Judgments and Fatwas

One of the most important and fruitful discussions in genre studies concerns the way rhetorical and discourse functions are realized through linguistic structures. For example, in his review of the literature on research articles, Swales (1990) shows how different sections in these texts (introduction, methods, results, and discussion) require different linguistic resources and notes in particular the variable distribution of features such as that-nominals,[1] the passive voice, the present tense, and the past tense. He points out, for instance, that that-nominals are very rare in the methods section and that the simple past occurs with highest frequency in the methods and results sections (Swales 1990:134–35).[2] While the author states that some of the proposed explanations for such findings should be viewed with caution, he admits that the statistical differences regarding the distribution of linguistic features across research article sections are "both striking and indicative" (Swales 1990:135). It is legitimate then to investigate relevant linguistic structures and the peculiar functions they fulfill in particular genres, as long as one is aware of possible limitations of the analyses proposed.

This chapter explores the main linguistic resources that serve to accomplish the discourse goals of each of the two genres under consideration, court judgments and fatwas. The investigation benefits from studies of language and the law that have dealt with the linguistic peculiarities of legal language and provided explanations for their occurrence. The long lists of such features that have been compiled for English and other Western

1. That-nominals are sentential complements of verbs such as *show* and *argue* that seem to occur in particular sections of research articles (Swales 1990:133–35). In the following example the portion in italics is a that-nominal: It has been shown *that the field of genre analysis has made significant progress.*

2. For example, Swales (1990:135) discusses data analyses that show that both the method and results sections of research articles favor the past tense, but they differ with respect to the use of the passive and the active.

languages (see discussion of English, French, and German legal language in Mattila 2006:159–254) serve as a point of reference for the detection of equivalent and similar items in Arabic legal texts. For example, it has been shown that, in order to "promote an aura of objectivity," judges favor impersonal constructions such as *this court finds* (instead of *I/we find*)[3] and that legalese exhibits a high frequency of binomial expressions such as *any and all, null and void,* or *cease and desist,* which may not have clear purpose but "may give an air of elegance" to legal texts (Tiersma 1999:64–68). Similar constructions are found in Arabic legal discourse, as in the couplets *'ikraah 'aw DaghT* "coercion or pressure" or *'amal 'aw xidma* "work or service" and the impersonal expression *qaDaaa lmajlis al'a'laa* "the Supreme Court rules" (Supreme Court 2006, 64–65:364–65). However, rather than simply identifying and illustrating multitudes of discrete elements such as these, the present discussion will focus instead on more global linguistic resources that contribute in important ways to the achievement of the main goals of the genres under consideration, court judgments and fatwas. These linguistic resources include the syntactic complexity manifested particularly in sentence structure and noun phrases, formulaic language, and the linguistic means of citing prior texts. It is hoped that this initial exploration will help to fine-tune relevant constructs and analytical procedures so that they can be applied with more efficiency to other structures.

1. SYNTACTIC COMPLEXITY

Various types of legal discourse, including legislative provisions, judicial opinions, and legal documents such as contracts, exhibit highly complex syntax with unusually long sentences involving a great deal of subordination, embedding, and conjoining (Cornu 1990; Bhatia 1993; Feteris 1999; Tiersma 1999; Mattila 2006). The following discussion uses excerpts from the court judgments and fatwas to illustrate and account for the degree of sentence complexity involved. This discussion is then extended to the special case of complex noun phrases, which have been shown to be quite frequent and greatly valued in legal discourse because they allow for concision and precision (Bhatia 1992).

1.1. Sentence Structure

The discussion of sentence complexity considers the court judgments first before turning to the fatwas. As shown in an earlier study (Fakhri 2002) and

3. French judgments also favor the impersonal tone whereby judges refer to themselves collectively as *La Cour* "the Court."

strongly corroborated by the present study (see section 3 of chapter 3), the organization of Moroccan judgments has been borrowed from the French model where the court opinion, especially that of the *Cour de Cassation*,[4] is formulated as a single sentence, with various adjuncts and subordinate clauses laying out the different grounds put forth by the court followed by the enunciation of the court's ruling at the end (Cornu 1990; Lasser 1995). Example (1) represents the basic structure of a judgment rendered by the French *Cour de Cassation*, which is cited in the French original in Mendegris and Vermelle (1996:40) and discussed in Fakhri (2002:165). Appendix C gives the French judgment with an English translation.

(1)	La Cour	The Court
	Attendu que . . . ; que . . . ; que . . .	Considering that . . . ; that . . . ; that . . .
	attendu que . . . ; que . . .	considering that . . . ; that . . .
	Mais attendu que . . .	But considering that . . .
	Par ces motifs rejette . . .	For these reasons rejects . . .

Setting aside boilerplate language[5] at the beginning and at the end of the text, a similar formulation of the Moroccan Supreme Court judgment as single-sentence structure is adopted as shown in (2).

(2)	Haythu yustafaadu . . . 'anna . . .	Considering that it is indicated that . . .
	Haythu 'innahu . . .	Considering that . . .
	Haythu 'inna . . .	Considering that . . .
	lihaadhihi al'asbaab	For these reasons
	qaDaa al majlisu binaqDi . . .	The Court rules to annul . . .
		(Supreme Court 2006, 66:207)

Within the single-sentence structure of the judgment, the segments that introduce the different grounds may themselves be quite long and complicated. For instance, one of these segments includes 235 words, fifteen tokens of the coordinating conjunction *wa* "and," thirteen complement clauses, four relative clauses, and two causal clauses (Supreme Court 2006, 64–65:229). The depth of embedding of different constituents also

4. The *Cour de Cassation* is the highest French jurisdiction. Its main function is to insure correct application of the rule of law by lower courts, and it considers both penal and civil matters brought before it.

5. Boilerplate language at the beginning of the judgment includes formulas such as *wa ba'da almudaawalati Tibqan lilqaanuun* "after deliberation according to the law." At the end of the judgment, routine statements are made concerning the registration of the decision in official court records and the composition of the court.

contributes significantly to the syntactic complexity of the court judgments. Excerpt (3), which represents only the first portion of a very long sentence, shows a conditional clause embedded in a relative clause which in turn is embedded in the main clause. The latter itself is conjoined to a previous clause as indicated by the conjunction *wa* "and" at the beginning of the excerpt and to a following clause with still more dependent clauses attached to it. The use of boldface in the excerpt is intended to facilitate the location of these features.

(3) . . . **wa** ’axDa’at [almaHkama] annaazilata limuqtaDayaati almaadda 419 min mudawwanati attijaara **allatii** ’a‘Tat lilmaHkama assulTa lita-Hdiidi ’ujrati assamasaar **’idhaa** lam tuHaddad bittifaaqin ’aw ‘urf **wa** ’istab‘adat tawSiyyata jam‘iyyati alwukalaa’i al‘aqaariyyiin liwilaayati faas almu’arraxa fii 20/5/01 **likawnihaa** laa tarqaa ’ilaa martabati alqa-anuun **Hatta** yumkinu ’i‘timaaduhaa kawathiiqatin litaHdiidi ’ujrati assamsaar . . .

. . . **and** [the court] subjected the case to the stipulations of article 419 of the Code of Commerce **which** give the court the authority to determine real estate agents' fees **if** they have not been fixed by agreement or custom **and** discarded the recommendation of the Association of Real Estate Agents of the Governorship of Fez dated 5/20/2001 **because** it does not rise to the status of law **so that** it could be considered as a document for determining real estate agents' fees . . .

(Supreme Court 2006, 66:144)

The syntactic complexity in court judgments has been accounted for in several ways. In general terms, Mattila (2006:90) traces the sentence complexity found in Western legal discourse back to "the old language of royal chancelleries" in Europe and to the "Latin notarial profession." While it is clear that the Moroccan court judgments are influenced by the French model, it would be far-fetched to go further and attribute their linguistic features to the same origins mentioned by Mattila. Tiersma (1999), on the other hand, provides a more "universal" account of syntactic complexity that can be extended to the Arabic data. He suggests that "a motivation of lengthy sentences is the desire to place all information on a particular topic into a self-contained unit" (Tiersma 1999:56). According to this view, the formulation of the judgment as a single sentence serves to highlight the closeness of different grounds and the verdict and reinforces the logical relation between them so as to preclude any ambiguity. Such logical relation is further strengthened by the use of the phrases *Par ces motifs* in French and *lihaadhihi al’asbaab* in Arabic "for these reasons" that link the grounds to the verdict in an explicit fashion.

Lasser (1995) provides a rather interesting contextual account for the single-sentence structure of court judgments based on the political history of the French governmental system where a rigid separation of powers has been established in order to rein in a distrusted judiciary and shore up the supremacy of the legislature. The role of the judges in such a system is thus limited to strict applications of the rule of law, which precludes any innovative interpretations of legal rules. In Lasser's (1995:1341) terms, the rigid single-sentence structure of court judgments helps to constrain the contribution of judges:

> The formal, single-sentence structure of the French judicial decision resists any discourse that might hamper its smooth grammatical flow. Any discussion that would introduce uncertainty or debate into the text of the decision, thereby tending to complicate the grammar of the sentence, conflicts with the very structure of the decision. . . . The French decision, in its paradigmatic form, possesses a univocal quality that denies the possibility of alternative perspectives, approaches, or outcomes.

It is highly unlikely that the modeling of the Moroccan Supreme Court judgments after their French counterpart has been motivated by the same governance concerns as those attributed to French system. It is rather the practical, socioeducational reasons discussed earlier that appear to have facilitated the adoption of the French model. Nonetheless, it is not unreasonable to expect that the use of the rigid grammatical structure in the Moroccan judgments produces similar effects of constraining what judges can do when drafting their decisions. In other words, because of this adopted structure, Moroccan judges are compelled to formulate their opinions in consistently predictable ways: they have to refer to relevant laws and make sure that their arguments fit together as a whole and lead to the final verdict in a logical manner, consistent with the explicit proposition expressed by the required phrase *lihaadhihi al'asbaab* . . . "for these reasons. . . ." Adherence to such practice should, in principle, discourage spurious manipulations of the rule of law and promote auspicious administration of justice by drawing attention to, and making suspect, any deviation from the customary formal structure of the judgment. If this holds, such an unintended consequence of borrowing French legal rhetoric illustrates positive effects of cross-cultural contacts and may in part explain the appeal of this rhetorical practice and its maintenance in the Moroccan judiciary.[6]

6. Bhatia (1993:14) suggests that specialists with expert knowledge of the conventions of a particular genre may, for personal reasons, deviate from these conventions, but only to a certain degree because such deviations can make their text appear odd.

The consistency of the sentence complexity observed in court judgments contrasts with sentence structure in the fatwas, which exhibit stretches of discourse with varying degrees of syntactic complexity. This variation is due in part to the function of the discourse considered. Recall that, following Goffman's (1981) insights discussed earlier, shifts in footing from mufti to teacher, counselor, or narrator are associated with changes in the kind of language used. The mufti may present legal arguments, explain relevant concepts, and relate ancient stories to make a point. These different discourse functions constitute basic elemental genres (Hyland 2007:28) which are combined in the fatwas and which require different types of syntax. For example, argumentation generally calls for complex syntax, whereas the narration of events is often realized through sequences of simple clauses (Labov 1972; Ochs 1997; van Eemeren et al. 1997). Examples (4) and (5), which illustrate argumentation and explanation respectively, are syntactically more complex than (6), which recounts a story.

(4) 'idhaa tarattaba 'alaa tawassuTi man shafa'a laka fii alwaDhiifati Hirmaanu man huwa 'awlaa wa 'aHaqqu bitta'yiini fiihaa min jihati alkifaaya al'ilmiyya allatii tata'allaqu bihaa . . . faashshafaa'atu muHarramatun li'annahaa Dhulmun liman huwa 'aHaqqu bihaa . . .
If the intervention of the person who supports you to obtain employment results in denying such employment to a person who has more academic qualifications which are pertinent to the job . . . then the intervention is prohibited because it is an injustice toward a more deserving person . . .

(The Committee in Rifaa'ii 1988, 3:332)

(5) wa 'ajru almithl 'aw 'iwaDu almithl alldhii dhakarahu fuqahaa'unaa yuqSadu bihi al'ajru al'aadilu alladhii yastaHiqquhu mithluh fii muqaabili 'amalihi ma'a muraa'aati kulli aDhDhuruuf wa al'awaamil allatii lahaa 'alaaqatun bitaHdiidi qiimati al'amal . . .
And comparable wage or comparable compensation which is mentioned by our religious scholars refers to a fair wage that an equally qualified worker is entitled to as a compensation for his work, with consideration of all the circumstances and factors which are related to the determination of the value of the work . . .

(Qaradawi 1981, 1:509)

(6) . . . fa qaala lahu sa'd: yaa 'axii 'innii min 'akthari annaasi 'amwaalan fa ta'alaa 'ushaaTiruka maalii wa 'indii zawjataani 'unDhur 'ilaa 'awqa'ihaa fii qalbik 'uTalliquhaa lak . . . wa 'indii daaraan taskunu 'iHdaahumaa wa 'anaa 'askunu al'uxraa . . . qaala lahu [Ibn 'awf]: yaa 'axii baaraka allaahu laka fii maalik wa fii 'ahlik wa fii daarik. 'innamaa 'anaa 'imru'un taajir, fadulluunii 'alaa assuuq.

> . . . And Sa'd said to him [Ibn 'Awf]: O brother, I have more wealth than most; so let me share it with you; and I have two wives; so see the one you like and I will divorce her for you . . . ; and I have two houses; you live in one and I live in the other . . . He [Ibn 'Awf] said to him: O brother, may God bless your wealth, and your family, and your house; but I am a merchant; just show me the market.
>
> (Qaradawi 1981, 1:521)

Examples (4) and (5) include several instances of relativization, a conditional clause, and a causal clause. On the other hand, excerpt (6), which is intended to illustrate both merchants' solidarity and self-reliance, exhibits a high degree of orality typical of narrative discourse, and comprises a sequence of simple independent clauses conjoined with *wa* "and." The co-occurrence in fatwas of stretches of discourse with varying degrees of syntactic complexity reflecting different discourse functions such as narration and argumentation is not an unusual phenomenon. In fact, most notably, Labov's (1972) seminal work on narration amply documents syntactic variation in the same story. One of the most insightful findings of this research is that narrators do not simply recount what happened but tend to evaluate their stories by providing commentary on the reported events. Such evaluations exhibit more syntactic complexity (e.g., causal clauses and conditionals) than other parts of the narrative where simple conjoined clauses describe sequences of events.[7] In sum, this discussion of sentence structure clearly indicates that court judgments exhibit a high level of syntactic complexity similar to their French origin. The fatwas, on the other hand, include a mixture of simple sentence structures and more complex ones. This discussion of syntactic complexity would be incomplete without also considering the particular case of complex noun phrases, given the importance of their functions in legal discourse.

---

7. Examples (a) and (b) illustrate the syntactic variation found in narratives.

(a) This guy punched me
and I punched him
and the teacher came in
and stopped the fight
(Labov 1972:360)

(b) Well, 'cause you have heard of people going to a funeral and getting killed themselves before they got there and that is the first thing that came to my mind.
(Labov 1972:372)

In (a) simple clauses conjoined by *and* report the sequence of events that happened. In (b), on the other hand, the narrator, who was telling about a near- accident she had on her way to a funeral, comments on why she was frightened. Her evaluation includes more complex syntax involving a causal clause, a temporal clause, and a relative clause in the same utterance.

1.2. Complex Noun Phrases

Before discussing the most salient functions of complex noun phrases in the court judgments and fatwas, I will first make brief comments on the formal structure of complex noun phrases and summarize Bhatia's (1992) work on their function in discourse, since these studies are used as the primary source for interpreting the data under consideration. The discussion presented here is partly based on Fakhri (2012a), which also includes analysis of nominalization in legislative provisions.

The syntactic complexity of noun phrases results from the presence of different types of modifiers added to the head noun. Such modifiers may consist of one or more words, typically adjectives, a phrase (e.g., a prepositional phrase), or even a complete clause as in the case of relativization. The English and Arabic examples (7) and (8) illustrate these types of modification.

(7) The young man with the hat who just left

(8) zawju almar'ati alfaransiyyati alladhi daxala alqism
The French women's husband who entered the classroom

An important source of noun phrase complexity that has attracted the attention of linguists is nominalization, defined by Givón (2009:66) as "the process via which a finite verbal clause . . . is converted into a noun phrase." For instance, the finite clause in (9) can be nominalized, resulting in the complex noun phrase in (10).

(9) She knows mathematics extensively.

(10) Her extensive knowledge of mathematics

As Givón (2009) shows, the study of nominalization is quite insightful because it is related to the issue of finiteness and its variable realization across languages. Finiteness is viewed not as a discrete either-or feature, but rather as involving different degrees illustrated in (11), which is adapted from Givón (2009:67). The least finite construction is the noun phrase in (11a), and the most finite one is the full-fledged sentence in (11d), with (11b) and (11c) showing intermediate degrees of finiteness.

(11) a. Her good knowledge of math
b. Her knowing math well
c. Knowing math as well as she did
d. She knew math well.

This linkage between nominalization and finiteness leads to an interesting insight concerning language typology: some languages tend to be nominalizing languages, whereas others favor finiteness, with extreme types characterized by Givón (2009:68) in the following terms:

> The broadest cross-language typological distinction in finiteness is the seeming chasm between extreme nominalizing and extreme finite languages. In the first type, all subordinate clauses are nominalized, at least historically. Only main clauses display fully finite structure. In the second, no clause type at all is nominalized, and all clause-types are fully finite.

This typological distinction is worth exploring further to figure out the possibility of its usefulness in distinguishing legal genres such as court judgments from other professional or academic genres.

One of the most focused and explicit treatments of the use of nominal expressions in academic and professional discourse appears in Bhatia (1992, 1993). The author highlights the importance of this topic in these terms:

> Complex nominal expressions of various kinds are typically associated with academic and professional genres and have gained a certain degree of notoriety in recent years. To the specialist community they are a useful linguistic device to bring in text cohesion, facilitating reference to (associated) technical concepts already mentioned; however, to the non-specialist outsider this is nothing but jargon. (Bhatia 1993:148)

Bhatia (1993:148–50) distinguishes three types of nominal expressions: complex nominal phrases comprising a series of attributes, typically adjectives before the head noun, as in (12); compound nominal phrases which include a sequence of nouns (and occasionally adjectives), as in (13); and, finally, nominalizations (see discussion above).

(12) The world's first packless, cordless, lightweight, compact, integrated videolight

(13) Airport building roof truss failures

The functions of these nominal expressions are determined by the purpose of the genre in which they appear. In product advertisements, complex nominal phrases serve to describe and positively evaluate the product being promoted by providing "a number of syntactic slots in which to insert suitable modifiers to accomplish the right kind of product-detailing" (Bhatia 1993:151). In scientific writing, compound nominal phrases are used to express new concepts and subsequently refer to them in a concise fashion, thus sparing the writer "tedious repetitions of long descriptions" (Bhatia 1993:153). Nominalizations are often used in legislative discourse to achieve a level of conciseness necessary for the formulation of comprehensive legal rules. Bhatia (1992:226) shows how verbal expressions are nominalized and then integrated into still more complex nominal structures as in (14), which is taken from the 1970 Wills Act of the Republic of Singapore.

(14) No obliteration, interlineation, or other alteration made in any will after the execution thereof shall be valid or have any effect . . .

The nominalizations in (14) aim at avoiding lengthy descriptions of various actions, using instead the series of single-term nominals "obliteration," "interlineation," "alteration," and "execution" to refer in a comprehensive manner to as many aspects of human behavior as necessary. Bhatia (1992:227) elaborates on the purpose of such highly nominal style in legislative writing:

> The use of nominal rather than verbal elements is likely to provide "more mileage" as it were to the legislative writer when one of his main concerns is to be able to cram detail after detail and qualification after qualification in his legislative sentence.

The use of complex noun phrases in the court judgments appears to be motivated by concerns for conciseness and certainty of reference similar to those discussed above. This issue is discussed first before turning to the special case of nominalizations in the fatwas.

The court judgments exhibit a high frequency of complex noun phrases, with varying degrees of complexity and types of modification. In the noun phrase (15) the head noun *addaa'inu* "the creditor" is followed by the attribute *almurtahinu* "garantor" and a relative clause that includes three nominalizations (*'ish'aar* "notification," *arraghbati* "intention," and *fasxi* "rescission"), a prepositional phrase, and multiple instances of *'iDaafa,* or the construct state.[8]

8. *'iDaafa* constructions consist of a sequence of two nouns as in *kitaabu alwaladi* "book of the boy" where the first noun is the construct state. The construct state is part of a three-way distinction regarding the form of nouns, the other two being the indefinite state signaled by the [n] (or *tanwiin*) in *kitaabun* "a book" and the definite state indicated by the addition to the noun of the definite marker *al* as in *alkitaabu* "the book."

(15) addaa'inu almurtahinu alladhii yanbaghii 'ish'aaruhu min Tarafi maaliki al'aqaari bi arraghbati fii fasxi 'aqdi alkiraa'
The guarantor creditor who should be given notification by the owner of the real estate regarding the latter's intention of rescission of the lease

(Supreme Court 2006, 66:218)

Crucial evidence for the preference of nominal style in court judgments comes from cases where the writer has a choice between nominal expressions as in (16) and their equivalent verbal expressions as in (17).

Linguistic Properties of Court Judgments and Fatwas

(16) ya'iibu aTTaa'inu 'alaaa lqaraari almaT'uuni fiih taHriifa minHati al'aqdamiyya.
The petitioner faults the contested court decision with misconstruing the seniority bonus.

(Supreme Court 2006, 64–65:364)

(17) ya'iibu aTTaa'inu 'alaa alqaraari almaT'uuni fiih 'annahu Harrafa minHata al'aqdamiyya.
The petitioner faults the contested court decision in that it has misconstrued the seniority bonus.

Both sentences in (16) and (17) are acceptable; however, the nominal option in *taHriifa minHati al'aqdamiyya* "misconstruing the seniority bonus" is by far the most frequently used. By contrast, the fatwas do not exhibit such overwhelming preference for nominalization, with both verbal and nominal expressions attested in the data as suggested in (18) and (19).

(18) laa yajuuzu al'amalu fii mithli haadhihi albunuuk . . .
Work in these banks is not permissible . . .

(Ibn Baz in Rifaa'ii 1988, 2:280)

(19) laa yajuuzu laka 'an ta'mala fii maHallaatin tabii'u alxumuur . . .
It is not permissible for you to work in places that sell alcoholic beverages . . .

(Ibn Baz in Rifaa'ii 1988, 3:351)

In (19) the complement of *yajuuzu* is the clause with a subject, "you," and a verb, "work," whereas in (18) the nominalized form *al'amal* "the work" is used. It is worth noting that in some instances, as in (20) below, verbal expressions include a 'generic' noun such as *'insaan* "person" serving as agent that has little informative value.

(20) yajuuzu li al'insaani 'an yabii'a sil'atan . . .
It is permissible for a person to sell a merchandise . . .
(The Committee in Shawadfi 1987:85)

Dispensing with the noun *'insaan* "person" in (20) and using nominalization instead does not lead to loss of information, as indicated by the resulting sentence *yajuuzu bay'u sil'atin* "the sale of a merchandise is permissible."

Complex noun phrases in the court judgments often serve three main functions that are crucial for achieving the goals of these texts. First, they are necessary for achieving precision of reference to legal texts as in (21a) where the noun phrase includes a numeral modifier, a prepositional phrase, and *'iDaafa.* Complex noun phrases may be embedded in a larger syntactic frame, resulting in an even more complex noun phrase as shown in (21b), which includes the noun phrase in (21a).

(21) a. almaadda 419 min mudawwanati attijaara
Article 419 of the Code of Commerce
b. suu'u taTbiiqi muqtaDayaati al maadda 419 min mudawwanati attijaara
The faulty application of the provisions of article 419 of the Code of Commerce
(Supreme Court 2006, 66:142)

Second, noun phrase complexity is motivated by robust advocacy that requires the use of multiple evaluative terms to strengthen one's position. A frequent noun phrase (or slight variations thereof) used in petitions for the annulment of lower courts' decisions is given in italics in (22), which describes the justification of a court decision as unsound, insufficient, and, for all practical purposes, null.

(22) ya'iibu aTTaalibu 'alaa alqraari almaT'uuni fiih . . . *suu'a wa nuqSaana atta'liili almuwaazii li'in'idaamih.*
The petitioner faults the contested decision with unsoundness and insufficiency of justification equivalent to its absence.
(Supreme Court 2006, 66:325)

The reason given for seeking the annulment of the court decision could have been stated more succinctly as *nuqsaanu atta'liili* "insufficient justification," for example; instead it is more forcefully expressed by the addition of the terms *suu'a* "unsoundness" and *almuwaazii li'in'idaamih* "equivalent to its absence." The resulting lengthy noun phrase is routinized to capture the notion of "bad justification" that is repeatedly invoked as a rationale for invalidating court decisions (see discussion of formulaic language below).

Third, complex noun phrases are used for the purpose of efficient anaphoric reference by condensing detailed information mentioned earlier through the process of nominalization. The italicized noun phrase in (23) summarizes the content of a previous section in the judgment which has detailed the negligent conduct of a bank and the prejudice it has caused to one of its client firms. The bank, in violation of its agreement with the client, kept promissory notes instead of presenting them for payment by a certain date to a third party, which resulted in important business losses for the firm.

(23) 'inna adda'waa allatii 'aqaamathaa almaTluubatu tahdifu 'ilaa *alHukmi 'alaa albanki bi'adaa'ihi lahaa ta'wiiDan 'ani aDDarari alldhii tasabbaba fiihi lahaa bi'adami taqdiimihi alkumbiaalaat almusallama lahu lial'istixlaaS fii 'aajaalihaa almuHaddada.*

The lawsuit brought by the respondent aims at *ordering payment by the bank of compensation for the prejudice it has caused by not presenting for payment and on time the promissory notes submitted to it.*

The noun phrase complement of *tahdifu 'ilaa* "aims at" includes the following nominalizations: *alHukm* "ordering," *'adaa'* "payment," *taqdiim* "presentation," and *'istixlaaS* "disbursement."

Regarding nominalizations in the fatwas, their most important and interesting function is to create legal concepts that can then be easily and unambiguously referred to in order to support muftis' legal opinions. The source of such nominalizations is often the Quran or hadith, as shown in the following examples, where the nominalizations are given in "a" and the sentential source is given in "b."

(24) a. atta'aawunu 'alaa al'ithmi wa al'udwaan

Cooperation on sin and transgression

b. wa ta'aawanuu 'alaa albirri wa attaqwaa wa laa ta'aawanuu 'alaa al'ithmi wa al'udwaan.

And cooperate on piety and devoutness and do not cooperate on sin and transgression.

(Quran, Surat almaa'ida:3)[9]

9. *Sura* or *surat* is a chapter from the Quran. Thus *surat almaa'ida* is "the chapter on the table" and *surat attawba* is "the chapter on repentance."

(25) a. al'amru bi alma'ruufi wa annahyu 'ani almukar
The promotion of virtue and the prevention of vice
b. almuuminuuna wa almuuminaatu ba'Duhumu 'awliyaa'u ba'D yaamuruuna bialma'ruufi wa yanhawna 'ani almunkar.
Men and women believers are each other's support; they promote virtue and prevent vice.
(Quran, Surat attawba:71)

(26) a. bay'u almuslimi 'alaa almuslim
The sale by a Muslim at the expense of another Muslim ("unfair competition")
b. laa yabi' ba'Dukum 'alaa bay'i ba'D.
No one shall sell at the expense of somebody else's sale.
(hadith cited in Al-Moumni 1998:165)

The complexity of these types of nominalizations stems from the retention of much of the original text to form the legal concept. Thus, instead of using a single term such as *almushaaraka* "complicity" to capture succinctly the prohibition expressed in (24), the formulation of the legal concept in (24a), apart from changing the verb *ta'aawannuu* "cooperate" into the nominal *atta'aawunu* "cooperation," keeps the same structural elements: *atta'aawunu 'alaa al'ithmi wa al'udwaan* "cooperation on sin and transgression." A possible motivation for retaining original forms is to stress the Quranic origin of the concept and, thus, its authority and in this case the gravity of the offence. The retention of Quranic forms in (25a) serves to highlight the desirability and the obligation to promote virtue and prevent vice.

As in the case of court judgments mentioned earlier, the complexity of the noun phrases considered in (24–26) above is often augmented by their insertion in even more complex syntactic frames as shown in (27). The legal concept (the noun phrase in boldface) is included in a longer noun phrase (in italics) that contains additional elements: a quantifier, a prepositional phrase, and a case of *'iDaafa*.

(27) . . . Harrama [al'islaamu] *kulla maDhharin min maDhaahiri* ***atta'aawuni 'alaa al'ithmi wa al'udwaan.***
Islam forbids *any aspect of the manifestation of* ***cooperation on sin and transgression.***
(Qaradawi 1981, 1:529)

The above discussion shows that syntactic complexity, at both the sentence level and the phrase level, plays an important role in fulfilling the generic goals of court judgments and fatwas. The difference between the two genres in this regard lies in the fact that the syntax of the fatwas is more varied because of the discourse functions they comprise, with argumentation generally requiring a higher degree of syntactic complexity than narration, for example. It is important to note that this high level of syntactic complexity found in the current data is at odds with traditional characterization of Arabic discourse as essentially paratactic, relying for the most part on coordination to link various propositions and construct loosely cohesive texts.

2. FORMULAIC LANGUAGE

The aim of the following discussion is to show how formulaic language expresses important functions that are necessary for the successful and efficient achievement of the purposes of the court judgments and fatwas. The discussion begins with a few preliminary remarks that outline some of the main issues in the study of formulaic language and its role in communication and provide context for the particular analyses of formulaic language in the data considered.

2.1. Preliminary Remarks

Formulaic language consists of more or less fixed sequences of words that express particular concepts or serve particular communicative and discourse functions, and tends to be associated with certain activities or communicative events. Examples of formulaic expressions often cited in the literature on the topic are *Hi! How are you?,* the frequent greeting formula, and *Why don't you . . . ?,* which serves to give advice or make a suggestion, as in *Why don't you call Dr. Smith?* Another example is the phrase *this is + name* (e.g., *This is John*), which is the typical way for callers to identify themselves when they leave messages on phone answering-machines (Aijmer 2007). In the domain of law, formulaic language is quite prevalent for many reasons, including conciseness, certainty of meaning, and protection of legal procedures (Mattila 2006; Tiersma 1999). The following are examples of legal formulas from Arabic, English, and French.

(28) albayyinatu ʿalaa almuddaʿii.
The burden of proof is on the plaintiff.

(29) I do hereby + Verb

(30) En fait de meubles, possession vaut titre.
For personal property, possession equals title.

European legal systems such as the French one have even retained Latin formulas such as *Actori incumbit probatio* "The burden of proof is on the plaintiff" (Cornu 1990).

The issue of formulaicity as a feature of natural languages has long been the subject of much debate. In Chomsky's tradition, formulaic language is considered marginal in understanding language and language processing; rather, what is valued is the generative capacity of language and the ability of speakers to use a finite set of rules to create an infinite number of novel sentences. This is a fundamental property of "generative grammar," a term coined by Chomsky "to refer to a precise formulation of the combinatorial principles that characterize a speaker's competence" (Jackendoff 2002:40). However, citing seminal work of Ferdinand de Saussure, Edward Sapir, and Leonard Bloomfield, Wray and Perkins (2000:11) cogently argue that the importance of formulaic expressions in language production and comprehension has also been recognized and propose a role for both "creative and holistic" processes in language use:

> Our view is that the best deal in communicative language processing is achieved by the establishment of a suitable balance between creative and holistic processes. The advantage of the creative system is the freedom to produce or decode the unexpected. The advantage of the holistic system is economy of effort when dealing with the expected.

There exists vast literature devoted to the study of formulaic language by adult native speakers and by first and second language learners (Coulmas 1981; Weinert 1995; Cowie 1998; Wray and Namba 2003; Skandera 2007). As many of these studies show, the investigation of formulaic language has often been confronted with a multitude of challenges and uncertainties. Wray and Perkins (2000:3) note, for example, the confusing proliferation of terms that refer to different types and subtypes of formulaic expressions. The authors were able to compile a list of more than forty terms used to characterize formulaic language "according to its form, function, semantic, syntactic and lexical properties, and its relationship with novel (analytic) language." Pawley (2007:13) lists fifteen questions and issues that, according to him, need to be addressed concerning the identification, classification, variability, and prevalence of formulaic language as well as its implication for language acquisition, language processing, and linguistic theory. In spite of these challenges, important and reliable insights on formulaic language have been gained by investigating rich sites of formulaic language such as "highly developed oral formulaic genres" (Pawley 2007). In this respect, studies of auctioneers' and sportscasters' talk (Kuiper 1996; Kuiper and Austin 1990) and the language of weather forecasts (Hickey and Kuiper 2000) have been quite fruitful. In particular, they show that these communicative events are characterized by highly formulaic discourse patterns and by the prevalence of formulaic expressions that allow for very fluent speech delivery, while at the same time facilitating comprehension because of their predictability. These few remarks will suffice as background for the discussion of the function of formulaic language in the court judgments and the fatwas.

2.2. The Functions of Formulaic Language in Court Judgments and Fatwas

Formulaic expressions tend to vary with respect to their indexical link to the communicative event or text in which they appear. As noted earlier, the expression *this is + name* is closely associated with answering-machine messages as a means of identifying oneself, whereas a phrase such as *thank you* can occur in a variety of contexts and serve diverse functions such as appreciation of a person's action or as a signal to end a phone call message, for example. Thus the discussion of formulaic expressions in the court judgments and fatwas begins with a brief mention of formulas that appear in these texts but that are not specific to them or to legal discourse in general. This is followed by an examination of wordlike formulaic expressions that serve to encode particular concepts, and then finally expressions whose function is discourse-oriented and consists in facilitating the organization of the structure of the two genres.

2.2.1. General Formulas

The expressions in (31) are examples of general formulas that appear in fatwas.

(31) a. kullu Saghiiratin wa kabiiratin
All things big and small
b. laa Hawla wa laa quwwata 'illaa bi allaah.
There is no might but that of God.
c. bighaDDi annaDhari 'an . . .
Without regard to . . .
d. bi al'iDaafati 'ilaa . . .
In addition to . . .
e. Name + raDiya allaahu 'anh
Name + may God be pleased with him
f. allaahu 'a'lam.
God knows best.

Expressions like these are not peculiar to legal discourse and can occur in a wide range of contexts. For example, the phrases in (31a–d) may appear in any type of text, with phrases like (31d) simply regulating textual organization. The structure in (31e), while somewhat more constrained, appears whenever a companion of the prophet is mentioned, whether in fatwas, sermons, or lectures on religious topics. The expression in (31f), *allaahu 'a'lam* "God knows best," may be found in different texts and even in face-to-face social interaction to mean "I don't know." In the fatwas, however, it is assigned a particular function; it serves as a coda, signaling the end of the text, with the additional connotation of modesty and humility on the part of the mufti.

In addition to examples such as those in (31), the fatwas often exhibit repeated syntactic frames that can be viewed as instances of idiosyncratic formulaicity resulting from the mufti's stylistic tendencies. Excerpt (32), taken from Qaradawi (1981, 1:524–25), shows phrases with open slots used repeatedly to express disapproval of greedy practices in commerce (*lima X* "why X") and to emphasize the religious duties that merchants should heed (*'an X* "from X"). The former pattern is repeated three times in (32a), and the latter seven times in (32b).

(32) a. lima al jash' wa lima aTTama' wa lima arribHu alfaaHish.
Why the cupidity and why the greed and why the exorbitant gains?
b. yajibu 'alaa attaajiri almuslim allaa tashghalahu tijaaratuh 'an waajibaatihi addiiniyya 'an dhikri allaah 'an aSSalaat 'an alHajj 'an albirri bialwaalidayn 'an Silati arraHim 'an al'iHsaani 'ilaa annaas . . .
Commerce should not distract the Muslim merchant from his religious duties, from God, from prayer, from pilgrimage, from caring for his parents, from contact with relatives, from helping others . . .

Repetitions like these are often viewed in Arabic discourse as preferred modes of arguing and persuading (Johnstone 1990; Hatim 1997; see also discussion in chapter 5). Note that the formulaic nature of the repeated phrases in (32b) is highlighted by the use of asyndeton, the omission of conjunctions, which is normally disallowed in Arabic. The omission of the expected *wa* "and" in this case is probably motivated by additional rhetorical emphasis. Such violations of syntactic rules are common in formulas; for example, in French the use of determiners in noun phrases is the norm, but in the phrase *en fait de meubles, possession vaut titre* mentioned earlier the nouns *possession* and *titre* are used without a determiner.

2.2.2. *Formulaic Expression of Legal Concepts*

Examples of the most frequent formulaic expressions used to express legal concepts or principles in the fatwas and court judgments are presented in (33) and (34), respectively.

(33) a. al'aSlu fii al'ashyaa'i al'ibaaHa
The root of things is permissibility (i.e., presumption of permissibility).
b. atta'aawunu 'alaa al'ithmi wa al'udwaan
Cooperation on sin and transgression
c. al'amru bialma'ruufi wa annahyu 'ani almunkar
The promotion of virtue and the prevention of vice

(34) a. nuqSaanu atta'liili almuwaazii li'in'idaamih
Insufficient justification equivalent to its absence
b. 'adamu al'irtikaazi 'alaa 'asaasin qaanuunii
Absence of a legal basis
c. alxarqu aljawharii lilqawaa'idi alqaanuuniyya
Substantial violation of rules of law
d. 'adamu arraddi 'alaa dufuu'
Absence of response to rebuttals

The repeated reference to these concepts in various fatwas and court judgments contributes to their routinization and to their formulation with a high degree of fixity and rigidity that characterize formulaic expressions. For example, in (33b) and (33c) the order of the phrases conjoined with *wa* "and" is never reversed, although Arabic syntax allows such modification. The concepts in (34), which serve to express reasons for invalidating lower court decisions by the Supreme Court, also appear in the same form in different judgments with occasionally slight modification such as the replacement in (34a) of the term *nuqSaanu* "insufficiency" with the term *suu'* "deficiency." The reference to these concepts consistently through the same formula has the advantage of guaranteeing certainty of meaning, since variation in form may only raise questions regarding the intended meaning.

The formulaic expression of the legal concepts also facilitates their processing. As discussed earlier, the formulation of concepts is often lengthy due to the desire to retain original authoritative language from the Quran and hadith in fatwas and to achieve strong advocacy in the court judgments. However, such lengthiness is not burdensome precisely because the resultant phrases have gained formulaic status and consequently are processed as a whole and do not require special effort in terms of either production or comprehension. This is all the more important that these concepts are frequently called upon because of their general applicability and of their potential to encompass diverse human conduct and various circumstances. Indeed, the concept of "cooperation on sin and transgression" has been invoked, for example, to prohibit work in restaurants that serve alcohol even if the work does not directly involve handling alcohol (e.g., storage or delivery to customers). As long as the establishment serves alcohol, employment there is prohibited because, it is argued, it is a form of cooperation on sin and transgression (Ibn Baz in Rifaa'ii 1988, 3:351). A similar argument based on the notion of "cooperation on sin and transgression" is made to prohibit all employment in banks practicing *ribaa* "usury" (Ibn Baz in Rifaa'ii 1988, 2:280). For its part, the concept of "the promotion of virtue and the prevention of vice" has been used in different cases to thwart all sorts of illegal activities and behaviors. It is invoked, for example, to assert the obligation of witnesses to a fraudulent sale to intervene and prevent the fraud (Shawadfi 1987:100).

2.2.3. *Formulas with Discourse Functions*

The court judgments and the fatwas differ greatly with respect to the use of formulaic expressions that mainly serve discourse functions. The court judgments, with a more rigorous structure adopted from the French judicial discourse (see discussion above), exhibit a higher frequency of such expressions than the fatwas. The list in (35) gives the main formulaic expressions in the same order in which they appear in the court judgments.

(35) a. Haythu ystafaadu min . . . 'anna . . .
Considering that it is indicated in [list of documents] that [summary of content]
b. fii sha'ni alwasiilati (al'ulaa/aththaaniya) . . .
Regarding the (first/second) ground . . .
c. Haythu . . .
Considering . . .
d. lihaaDhihi al'asbaab
For these reasons
e. qarrara almajlisu . . .
The court rules . . .

The function of (35a) is to introduce a summary of the case and the procedures, actions, and decisions taken so far by lower courts. This summary is based on the legal briefs and documents filed by the litigants. Items (35b–c) signal the claims made by the parties, most often the petitioner's: (35b) identifies the grounds put forth and (35c) outlines their content. These two phrases are repeated for all grounds that the court deems relevant for it to reach a decision. The phrase in (35d) serves as a link between the court's argumentation and its verdict stated in (35e). The language of the verdict is itself fairly routinized. In the case of rejection of the petition, the consecrated phrase is *qarrara almajlisu birafDi aTTalab wa taHmiili aTTaalibi aSSaa'ir* "The court rules to reject the petition and charges the petitioner with court costs." In the case of invalidation of the lower court decision, the following structure is used: *qarrara almajlisu binaqDi alqaraari almaT'uuni fiih wa 'iHaalati alqaDiyyati 'alaa* . . . "The court rules to invalidate the contested decision and send the case back to . . ."

In addition to their separate local functions, the formulas in (35), taken together, serve a more global discourse function: tracking the different components of the court judgment, with the concomitant enhancement of text cohesion and comprehension. This tracking function is similar to that of other linguistic mechanisms shown in previous research to track the distribution of information in discourse. For example, Givón's (1983) seminal work on topic continuity describes how tracking referents in discourse is achieved through intricate patterning of full noun phrases, pronouns, and zero anaphora. Thus for the first mention of a referent in discourse a full noun phrase is used; pronouns and zero anaphora are reserved for subsequent references. This pattern is adjusted, though, to avoid potential ambiguity of reference as in the case of introducing a new referent. The point of this patterning of referential forms is that the more continuous a referent is, the less the linguistic material required to trace it. In the same vein, Hopper (1979) demonstrates how the tracking of various events in narratives is realized through the tense-aspect system where, for example, progressive verb forms encode background information, while simple forms encode foreground events that push the story forward.

The expressions in (35) may not be readily recognizable as formulas in the same way as clichés and routines widely used in everyday social interaction; nevertheless, in the context of court judgments, they clearly have acquired formulaic status because of their frequency and formal rigidity, on the one hand, and because of the consistency of their function on the other, two criteria that have been commonly employed to identify formulaic language (Weinert 1995). For example, while the phrase *lihaadhihi ala'sbaab* "for these reasons" by itself and out of context may not be recognized as a formula, its use in the court judgments is definitely formulaic in that it appears in exactly the same form. Even minor variations such as *likulli haadhihi al'asbaab* "for all these reasons" or *lihaadhihi al'asbaab al'adiida* "for these numerous reasons" never appear in the data. Furthermore, functionally, this phrase occurs nowhere else in the judgments except before the enunciation of the verdict that it serves to introduce. We should note, however, that some judgments use instead the formula *min 'ajlih* "because of this." Other formulas may exhibit variability probably for stylistic reasons (e.g., to avoid monotonous repetitions). Thus in (35b) *fiisha'ni alwassiilati al'ulaa . . .* may be rendered as *biannisbati lialwasiilati al'ulaa . . .* "regarding/in relation to the first ground . . ."

Even though the fatwas exhibit less formulaicity than the court judgments regarding the organization of discourse, they often use the following sequences with open slots that serve as exponents of the two main moves in fatwas, answering the question and providing support: *yajuuzu . . . li . . .* "it is permissible to . . . because . . ." or *laa yajuuzu . . . li . . .* "it is not permissible to . . . because . . ." The excerpts in (36) illustrate these patterns.

(36) a. *yajuuzu* lial'insaani 'an yabii'a sil'atan mina aTTa'aami 'aw ghayrih 'ilaa 'ajalin ma'luum *li*qawlihi ta'aalaa: ". . . ."
It is permissible for a person to sell food or other merchandise with deferred payment because of God's saying: "Quran."
(Shawadfi 1987:85)

b. *laa yajuuzu* lilmuslimi 'an yashtarii sil'atan thumma yabii'ahaa qabla qabDihaa min man 'ishtaraahaa minh *li*qawli arrasuuli Sallaa allaahu 'alayhi wa sallama: ". . ."
It is not permissible for a Muslim to purchase a merchandise and then resell it before getting possession of it, because of the prophet's [honorific expression] saying: "Hadith."
(Al-Moumni 1998:165)

The above discussion of formulaic language highlights its multiple uses and advantages, which taken together constitute a major mechanism for achieving "efficient writing," a term used to characterize writing that can be easily produced and comprehended because of the consistency of its lexico-grammatical features and the predictability of its organizational patterns (Atkinson 2003). Thus in the data considered, the iterative formulation of particular legal notions insures certainty of meaning, a valuable goal in legal discourse. Also, the regularity of rhetorical patterns in the data enhanced by repeated usage of the same signposts leads to familiarity in organization and facilitates both text production and comprehension.

3. CITATIONS

Citations from the Quran and hadith in the fatwas and from codes and statutes in the court judgments are the most important means of providing support for the legal opinion provided. This section discusses the various linguistic devices that accomplish this important function and proposes contextual explanations for their choice. The discussion draws upon a previous study that I conducted on this topic (Fakhri 2008), and focuses on current findings that tend to corroborate the earlier ones. These concern the modes of reference to previous texts and the issue of attribution to authors, which will be addressed in section 3.2 and section 3.3, respectively. First, however, section 3.1 presents a brief overview of fundamental aspects of the use of citations in discourse that will serve as background for subsequent discussions.

3.1. The Use of Citations in Discourse

Citations involve the integration of previous texts into current ones and are subsumed under the general notion of intertextuality, according to which new texts are inevitably influenced by prior ones. The study of intertextuality has generated a great deal of interest in various disciplines such as philosophy, literary theory, rhetoric, and linguistics (Barthes 1977; Foucault 1984; Bakhtin 1986; Pennycook 1996; Hyland 2003). Some scholarship on intertextuality is theoretical, relating it to issues of creativity, originality, and authorship. Roland Barthes (1977:146) cited in Pennycook (1996:210) expresses the position that "a text is not a line of words releasing a single 'theological' meaning . . . but a multidimensional space in which a variety of writings, none of them original, blend and clash. The text is a tissue of quotations drawn from the innumerable centers of culture." Other studies of intertextuality such as those conducted within the field of composition and second language writing are of a more applied nature and discuss cultural and disciplinary differences regarding textual appropriation and how and when to cite (Polio and Shi 2010).

The realization of intertextuality through citations has important implications for the way knowledge is created and evaluated and for the status of participants involved in its creation. Foucault (1984:109) examines the development of the notion of authorship in the West and assesses the historical significance of citing others' texts in the following terms:

> In our civilization, it has not always been the same types of texts which have required attribution to an author. There was a time when the texts that we today

> call "literary" . . . were accepted, put into circulation, and valorized without any question about the identity of their authors. . . . On the other hand , those texts that we now would call scientific . . . were accepted in the Middle Ages, and accepted as "true," only when marked with the name of their author. "Hippocrates said," "Pliny recounts," . . . were the markers inserted in discourses that were supposed to be received as statements of demonstrated truth.

The point here is that the use of citations is meaningful and may affect the quality of the content of texts and how they are received. Current research on the topic indicates that citations are often carefully designed to serve specific purposes of authors who deliberately seek to produce certain effects on their audiences. In particular, the choice of linguistic means for citing previous texts often reveals authors' attitudes toward each other's works. For example, the choice of direct quotes or summaries may aim at giving prominence to the reported author or, alternatively, at emphasizing the reported message; the tense/aspect system may be manipulated to indicate various degrees of "psychological distance" from the cited material (e.g., simple past versus present perfect); the selection of certain reporting verbs such as "state," "assert," or "claim" may be motivated by the desire to evaluate previous scholarship, positively or negatively.

In order to provide more concrete illustrations of relevant aspects of citations, I will mention briefly the conclusions of select studies of academic discourse, which is one of the richest sites for data on citations. Tadros (1993) investigates the functions of citations in data from the fields of linguistics, sociolinguistics, and discourse analysis and attempts to determine whether differences in writers' purposes affect the way they use citations. The main finding of the study is that citations are avoided in order not to weaken the authority of the current writer, but utilized extensively when the purpose is to show gaps in the previous scholarship and to provide justification for the current research. Thompson and Yiyun (1991) deal in particular with the different types of reporting verbs in academic discourse and the significance of their selection. The data for their study come from article introductions in applied linguistics, geology, engineering and veterinary sciences. Their results indicate that the choice of reporting verbs depends on their denotation and evaluative potential, and reflects various degrees of the writer's commitment to or detachment from the reported material. In a more comprehensive study, Hyland (2000) examines citations in different academic disciplines, including physics, engineering, philosophy, and sociology. The study considers the surface forms of citations, the types of reporting verbs selected, and the integration of content from previous sources in the form of quotations, summaries, or generalizations. The analysis of the data shows that citation patterns vary across academic disciplines and tend to reflect the cognitive and cultural values of the communities they address. Insights from these studies of citations have been utilized to investigate fatwas and court judgments in Fakhri (2008). As mentioned earlier, the present discussion concentrates on aspects of citations in current data that corroborate the findings of this previous study. These include the modes of reference to previous texts and the attribution to authors.

3.2. Modes of Reference to Previous Texts in Court Judgments and Fatwas

The modes of reference to previous texts in the court judgments exhibit a great deal of variation ranging from simple identification of relevant laws and statutes to brief indications of their content and direct or indirect quotes of legal texts. On the other hand, the fatwas use direct quotes almost exclusively. In (37) the relevant law is identified simply by number, 112, and its source, the Code of Commerce.

(37) . . . xarqa almaaddati 112 min mudawwanati attijaara
. . . the violation of article 112 of the Code of Commerce
(Supreme Court 2006, 66:217)

The second mode of reference involves the addition of a brief mention of the content of the relevant rule of law as in (38), which specifies the type of damage covered by the article in question.

(38) . . . ’anna alfaSla 264 min [qaanuuni al’iltizaamaati wa al‘uquud] yata‘allaqu bi alxasaarati alHaqiiqiyyati wa alkasbi almafquud . . .
. . . article 264 of the Code of Obligations and Contracts concerns actual loss and loss of potential earnings . . .
(Supreme Court 2006, 66:253)

The third pattern is to quote legal texts directly or indirectly as in (39) and (40), respectively.

(39) . . . ’anna almaada 12 mina alqaanuuni almuHdithi lilmaHaakimi al’idaariyya tanuSSu ‘alaa maa yalii: “tu‘tabaru alqawaa‘idu almuta‘alliqatu bial’ixtiSaaSi min qabiili anniDhaami al‘aammi . . .”
. . . article 12 of the statute establishing administrative courts stipulates the following: “The rules concerning legal competence are considered a matter of public order . . .”
(Supreme Court 2006, 66:327)

(40) . . . binaa'an ʻalaa . . . alfaSli 1070 min [qaanuuni al'iltizaamaati wa alʻuquud] alladhii yanuSSu ʻalaa 'anna almuSaffii huwa alladhii yumaththilu ashsharika fii Tawri attaSfiyya.
. . . according to . . . article 1070 of the Code of Obligations and Contracts which stipulates that it is the liquidator who represents the company at the stage of liquidation.
(Al Milaf 2005, 6:360)

The variation observed in the court judgments (i.e., simple identification of relevant laws, brief mention of their subject matter, and direct and indirect quotes) is in sharp contrast with the consistency of type of citations in the fatwas, which rely overwhelmingly on direct quotations from the Quran and hadith. The fatwas include 104 direct quotes but only 9 cases of indirect quotes or brief mentions of content. By contrast, the entire corpus of the court judgments comprises only 12 direct quotes such as (39) above. The quotations in the fatwas are often introduced by a reporting clause with the verb *qaal* "say" solely or in conjunction with another reporting verb as in *thabata ʻani annabiyyi 'annahu qaal* "It was ascertained that the prophet said . . ." Verbs such as *thabata* "ascertain" or its synonym *SaHHa* are intended to enhance the authority of the hadith. Examples (41) and (42) illustrate these modes of reporting.

(41) qaala allaahu taʻaalaa: "wa man yattaqii allaaha yajʻal lahu maxrajan."
God [honorific expression] said: "God helps those devoted to Him."
(Ibn Baz in Rifaa'ii 1988, 3:351)

(42) thabata ʻani annabiyyi [honorific expression] 'annahu qaal: "man 'axadha 'amwaala annaasi yuriidu 'itlaafahaa 'atlafahu allaah."
It was ascertained that the prophet [honorific expression] said: "Whoever takes and wastes others' assets will be ruined by God."
(Shawadfi 1987:85)

This major difference between the court judgments and fatwas regarding the use of direct quotations can be accounted for in the following manner. Because of the nonbinding character of fatwas, the mufti needs to be very persuasive to ensure the acceptance of his opinion by the fatwa seekers. Thus in addition to appealing to the sense of piety and reverence that any reference to, or discussion of, content from the Quran and hadith creates in the community of believers, the fatwas, by selecting direct quotations, take advantage of the formal rhetorical sophistication and stylistic elegance of these texts to enhance their persuasive quality. In other words, the high degree of cohesion between the semantic content of the texts quoted and their formal properties (Jakobson 1960) is likely to have a positive effect on the readers of the fatwa and facilitates their acceptance of its recommendations. On the other hand, given that verdicts are enforceable, it seems sufficient for the court judgments to give a brief summary of the content of legal texts or to merely identify relevant laws by mentioning dates of publication and article numbers. Such brevity of reference is not only appropriate but even desirable. Indeed, extensive quotations of the law may be quite superfluous, since the argumentation in court judgments, especially those rendered by superior courts as is the case here, is primarily intended for lawyers and other legal experts who should be familiar with the content of legal texts and who, in case of doubt, possess the means and skills for consulting a variety of legal manuals or other sources available to them. In sum, the difference between fatwas and court judgments regarding how texts are quoted reflects a more general phenomenon often discussed in writing theories: the rhetorical organization of texts is at least partially shaped by the writers' awareness of audience expectations and characteristics.[10] In this instance, ordinary lay people and legal experts constitute different kinds of audiences that require different types of rhetoric. It is undeniable that even in the case of court judgments lay people are ultimately the parties concerned; however, given the complexity of legal language especially in cases brought in front of the Supreme Court, most of the time lawyers or other law professionals are called upon to mediate between them and the courts and hopefully explain to them the content of court decisions in terms they are able to understand.

3.3. Attribution to Authors

Fatwas and court judgments exhibit important differences regarding the attribution of the texts to which they refer. As shown in Fakhri (2008), the court judgments very rarely mention *almusharri'* "the legislator" as the source of the law, for the obvious reason that this would be superfluous. The practice of fatwas is quite different. In addition to mentioning God and the prophet when quoting from the Quran and hadith, the fatwas also refer to the chain of transmission of hadith, a phenomenon known as *'isnaad* "transmission." The hadith quoted in (43) is related to three sources, Ahmad, Muslim, and Jaabir, mentioned alongside the prophet.

10. This is particularly highlighted in social constructionist perspectives on writing where texts are considered to be shaped not only by writers' purposes and motives but also by audience characteristics and needs.

(43) limaa rawaahu 'ahmad wa muslim 'an jaabir raDiya allaahu 'anhu 'annahu qaal: qaala annabiyyu Sallaa allaahu 'alayhi wa sallam "'idhaa 'ibta'ta Ta'aaman fa laa tabi'hu Hattaa tastawfiih."
Because of what Ahmad and Muslim relate from Jaabir [honorific expression], who said that the prophet [honorific expression] said "if you were sold food do not resell it until you receive it in full."
(Shawadfi 1987:86)

Traditionally, *'isnaad* constitutes an intricate hadith transmission network, whose importance is described by Senturk (2005:37) in the following terms:

> The hadith transmission network was rooted in the attempts of Muslims to preserve the integrity of the teachings of the Prophet Mohammad, which, they soon realized, depended on a reliable transmission network. Forgery, motivated by sectarian and political interests or simply by mythical and fictional impulse, was against the interests of the companions of the prophet, the new converts, and the state.

The preservation of the quality of hadith and its integrity has always been an important goal in the development of Islamic thought. In his *Moqaddimah*, the fourteenth-century Islamic thinker and polymath Ibn Khaldun (1958) describes in some detail how hadith scholars, striving to insure the authenticity of the sayings of the prophet and to discard doubtful attributions, designed an elaborate system to determine the degree of reliability of the chain of transmission and to rank different hadith texts. For instance, a distinction is made between chains "skipping the first transmitter on Muhammad's authority (*mursal*), omitting one link (*munqaTi'*), omitting two links (*mu'Dal*) . . ." (Ibn Khaldun 1958, 2:450). The quality of the texts reported is also assessed, and in addition to hadith with unquestionable authenticity, namely *SaHiiH* "sound," "a text may be 'unusual' (*ghariib*), 'difficult' (ambiguous, *mushkil*) . . . or containing homonyms (*muftariq*), or containing homographs (*mukhtalif*)" (Ibn Khaldun 1958, 2:451).

While this original function of *'isnaad* (i.e., ensuring hadith integrity) may apply to the fatwas under consideration, the frequent mention of the prophet and the names of successive hadith transmitters seems also to be motivated, and perhaps even more so, by the mufti's desire to enhance the persuasive quality of his fatwa. Specification of authorship and sources is not necessary in the sense that the simple identification of the text as hadith is sufficient; indeed, in a few cases the sayings of the prophet are introduced by more general phrases such as *jaa'a fi alhadith* "it is mentioned in hadith . . ." Given the current context of fatwa issuing and the characteristics of the participants in this communicative event, the sometimes lengthy mention of the names of successive hadith transmitters in *'isnaad* is too detailed and esoteric to be informative for ordinary lay questioners with little or no background in *sharii'a* and the science of hadith in particular. In other words, it is not the case that the questioner is going to be able to assess the quality of the chain of transmitters in order to determine the appropriate reaction to adopt toward the fatwa. So the motivation behind the mention of the prophet and the various hadith transmitters must be something other than its information value. I would like to propose two complementary accounts for this finding, both of which are based on the nonbinding nature of the fatwa and on the fact that the questioner's decision to adhere to its recommendations or not would depend on its persuasive quality. First, the regular mention of the prophet and the hadith transmitters with the accompanying optative expressions such as *raDiya allaahu 'anh* "may God be pleased with him" must generate a sense of reverence and piety in the questioner, which is bound to enhance the emotional appeal or pathos of the fatwa. This is an important persuasive element in view of the fact that seeking a fatwa in the first place is a strong indication of a believer's need for spiritual guidance as to what would constitute appropriate Muslim conduct.

Second, the frequent use of *'isnaad* with long lists of hadith scholars can be taken, and probably legitimately so, as an indication of the mufti's erudition and competence, which should elevate his status or ethos in the eyes of the questioner. This persuasion device is reminiscent of what Latour (1987:131) calls black-boxing in academic discourse. In general, black-boxing consists in compiling "a large number of elements" and making them "act as one" in order to make one's writing convincing. As suggested by Block (1996: 70), black-boxing may be achieved through extensive citation of the research of other scholars, especially well-known ones, as a means of promoting one's own research. Preliminary findings from an ongoing empirical study suggest that the mention of hadith sources leads to positive evaluation of fatwas (Fakhri 2012b).[11]

---

11. The study seeks to determine the effects of mentioning sources on readers' perceptions of the quality of fatwas. For this purpose two modified versions of a fatwa taken from Shawadfi (1987:85–86) were constructed (see Appendix F). *Version 1* gives the opinion of the mufti and supports it with hadith that does not mention the sources, as shown in (a).

(a) . . . limaa jaa'a fi al'aHaadiithi attaaliya:
"'idhaa 'ishtarayta shay'an falaa tabi'hu Hattaa taqbiDh." . . .
. . . because of what was mentioned in the following Hadiths:
"If you purchase something, do not resell it until you get hold of it."

Version 2 gives the same opinion but mentions the hadith and its sources as in (b).

The need for similar elements of pathos and ethos, so to speak, is absent in the case of court judgments. Here the objective reference to legal texts themselves through dates and article numbers highlights the primacy of the law and connotes a high degree of detachment on the part of the court. Any indication of judges' subjectivity in the crafting of the text will be viewed with suspicion and even alarm. In brief, this concern for objectivity coupled with the redundancy of attribution to a diffuse entity such as "the legislator" precludes mention of authorship in the citations of court judgments.

SUMMARY

This chapter has focused on three main linguistic aspects (syntactic complexity, formulaic language, and the means of citing previous texts), and explored how these have been utilized to achieve important purposes of the texts considered. Sentence complexity in court judgments, modeled

---

(b) . . . limaa rawaahu Ahmad raHimahu allaah 'an Hakim Ibn Hizaam 'anna rasuula allaahi Sallaa allaahu 'alayhi wa sallama qaal:
" . . . 'idhaa 'ishtarayta shay'an falaa tabi'hu Hattaa taqbiDh." . . .
. . . because of what was reported by Ahmad may God have mercy on him from Hakim Ibn Hizaam that the messenger of God may God's blessing and peace be upon him said:
"If you purchase something, do not resell it until you have it in your possession."

Twenty-four subjects are asked to read and compare the two modes of support (hadith only and hadith plus sources) and decide which version they prefer and why. Except for one subject who mentions that he has no preference, all the subjects declare that they prefer *Version 2*, the one that includes both hadith and sources. The reasons they give for their preference are quite revealing. They all mention that the reason behind their choice is the presence of sources; some have added that these sources strengthen the authenticity of the hadith. A few went beyond these reasons and show appreciation of the transmitters and their reputation as reliable hadith scholars and that the prophet's companions mentioned as sources of hadith are reputed for their integrity and piousness as in (c).

(c) . . . wa arruwaatu mashhuudun lahum biriwaayati al'aHaadiithi aSSaHiiHati ka al'imaam muslim . . . 'an SaHaabatin mashhuudun lahum bi al'adli wa attaqwaa.
. . . And the hadith transmitters are reputed to report authentic hadith like Imaam Muslim . . . from the[prophet's] companions known for their integrity and piousness.

One of the subjects explicitly pointed out the positive effect of the mention of sources on the acceptance of the fatwa by questioners:

(d) . . . limaa tataDammanuhu min tafSiil wa 'idraaji assanad lilHadiith ashshay'u alladhii yataqabbaluhu assaa'ilu biqanaa'atin wa riDaa.
. . . because of the details it [the fatwa] contains and the inclusion of hadith sources, which the questioner receives with conviction and approbation.

after the French formulation of court decisions in a single-sentence structure, is shown to be motivated by the desire to strengthen the logical relationship among the different steps of the argumentation presented by the court. It has been argued that this type of syntactic structure is maintained by the Arabic law discourse community because it provides a useful readymade format that allows judgment drafters to concentrate on content rather than concern themselves with form. By contrast, sentence complexity in fatwas tends to vary depending on the discourse functions expressed in the texts, with narration showing less syntactic complexity than argumentation or explanation. These various functions, it has been suggested, are needed by the mufti to enhance the validity of his opinion given that fatwas are nonbinding. Syntactic complexity is also manifested in the structure of noun phrases through modification and nominalization. Noun phrase complexity is motivated by the concern for precision and conciseness of reference, the search for robust advocacy characteristic of adversarial legal procedures, and the retention in nominalized structures of material from the Quran and hadith in order to preserve its original authority.

The chapter has also discussed the use of formulaic language in the data, showing that it serves two main functions. First, it provides fixed expressions for referring repeatedly to legal notions and concepts, achieving thereby a high degree of certainty, a valued goal in legal settings. Second, in addition to enhancing textual coherence, the formulaic, routinized use of discourse patterns, with predictable signposts distributed along the texts, is beneficial for efficient drafting and for easy tracking of information displayed in the text.

Regarding the linguistic means of citing previous texts, it has been found that the fatwas are different from the court judgments in two important aspects. While the modes of citation in the court judgments vary from simple identification of texts to brief mention of content and quotes, the fatwas rely almost exclusively on direct quotes from the Quran and hadith. In contrast to court judgments, the citations of fatwas are also author-prominent, with frequent mentions of the prophet and his companions and various hadith transmitters. These differences are attributed to the mufti's rhetorical expertise in promoting his opinion through affective and spiritual appeal to audiences and by portraying himself as a competent, reliable, and thus trustworthy source of information about *sharii'a.*

Chapter Five
Conclusions and Implications

This study has used a genre analysis approach to investigate two related and culturally significant Arabic texts: court judgments and fatwas. The results of the analysis are discussed in chapters 3 and 4 and summarized at the end of each chapter. I will recall here some of the main insights and findings that are relevant to and that will facilitate later discussions in this chapter. These findings concern mostly the relation between features of the texts and properties of the context in which these texts are produced and used. Elements of contexts highlighted include the characteristics of participants and their relationships, and the purpose of the texts, which are considered central for understanding genre (Devitt 1989, 2004; Swales 1990; Bhatia 1993). The purpose of the fatwa to provide a nonbinding opinion has been shown to affect the modes of citing Quran and hadith that are designed to enhance the persuasiveness of the fatwa through affective appeal and through the portrayal of muftis as trustworthy providers of knowledge about *sharii'a* law. The lack of educational and social parity between questioners and muftis enables the latter to go beyond answering questions and offer unsolicited advice, explanation, and warnings, thus affecting the rhetoric of the fatwa. The latter is also shaped by the multiple social roles and professional duties of fatwa authors, who often serve as teachers and imams in mosques in addition to being muftis. These different roles, it has been argued, allow them to develop a multifaceted rhetorical expertise that manifests itself in the variety of different moves and discourse functions exhibited in the fatwas. Regarding the court judgments, their most salient feature, syntactic complexity, has been shown to be motivated by the need to state in an explicit manner the logical relations between propositions, thus achieving a high degree of certainty, a highly valued goal in legal discourse. It has also been argued that syntactic complexity is allowed by the characteristics of the audience to which the court judgments are addressed, namely lawyers and other law professionals, who possess expertise in legal rhetoric and jargon.

In this final chapter, I will elaborate on two main themes suggested by the study that have overarching implications for genre analysis and Arabic discourse and possibly other related areas of inquiry. The first theme concerns the significance of the rhetorical borrowing observed in the court judgments (section 1) and its impact on aspects of Arabic discourse (section 2). The second theme pertains to the effect on fatwas of the general sociocultural climate surrounding contemporary *'iftaa'*, which is intended to complement the accounts discussed earlier of the rhetorical patterns identified and to provide a broader and more complete view of this peculiarly Islamic genre (section 3). In addition to these main themes, I will make brief remarks on cultural traits revealed by the generic practices observed (section 4), before providing in the final section (section 5) several suggestions regarding the type of future inquiries needed to fill in gaps in our current understanding of the issues discussed, highlighting in particular the necessity to take advantage of insights from genre analysis research in order to address these issues in a meaningful fashion.

1. THE SIGNIFICANCE OF ADOPTING THE FRENCH MODEL IN THE COURT JUDGMENTS

In order to understand the significance of the rhetorical borrowing shown in the analysis of court judgments, it is necessary to consider some relevant aspects of the sociolinguistic situation of Arabic. As noted in chapter 1, this situation is quite complex and exhibits extensive linguistic variation that different scholars have over the years attempted to capture by proposing different models and a multitude of taxonomies (Ferguson 1959; Blanc 1960; Mitchell 1986; Holes 2004; Bassiouney 2009). This sociolinguistic situation is further complicated by the contact of Arabic and other languages. An important aspect of this language contact that is relevant to the present discussion is the substantial amount of borrowing from French into Moroccan Arabic. As mentioned in chapter 1, the borrowed words are used in informal everyday interaction, especially in domains introduced with the arrival of the French in Morocco such as those of sports and automobiles (Heath 1989).

The present study focuses on an altogether different type of borrowing, namely the wholesale borrowing of generic patterns from the French court judgments into the Arabic ones. It has been argued that the striking similarity between the French and Arabic court judgments regarding the rhetorical patterns and the types of phrases used preclude the possibility that these features have developed independently in the two languages.

As mentioned earlier, this argument is further supported by the adoption of educational policies that have introduced French–Arabic bilingual curricula in law faculties where future judges, lawyers, and other law professionals are exposed to the French rhetorical tradition, especially as these curricula include explicit instruction on legal rhetoric (e.g., exercises in *commentaire d'arrêt* "commentary on court judgment").[1] The systematic study of this type of rhetorical borrowing is an important contribution to the research on language contact situations, which has traditionally focused on lexical and syntactic interlingual influences.

The borrowing of French rhetorical moves documented here is even more significant for genre analysis research. First, genre studies have proposed that genres emerge as responses to recurrent communicative situations recognized and established as valuable modes of social interaction (Miller 1984; Atkinson 1999; Hyland 2000; Devitt 2004). The repeated involvement of various participants in such situations leads to the negotiation and the creation of preferred modes of communication which are then conventionalized into genres with specific rhetorical and linguistic features aimed at achieving generic goals. Such features gain acceptance and become used widely because they facilitate the task of producing and comprehending tokens of the genre. This study identifies a different type of genre emergence, since clearly the rhetorical patterns in the Arabic court judgments did not emerge as a result of the usual process of "internal" development of a generic practice; instead, rhetorical patterns have been "transplanted," so to speak, from French into Arabic judicial discourse as a useful and efficient readymade rhetorical apparatus.[2] However, as is the case of the "normal" emergence of genres, this rhetorical borrowing is not disassociated from the prevailing sociocultural context of the Moroccan judiciary. As suggested by Hyland (2000:162) regarding academic argumentation, generic conventions "draw on community values influenced by the ideologies and power relations which dominate current socio-economic realities." It is the socioeconomic realities of twentieth-century Morocco, the country's search for modernity, and the

1. The transfer of the French patterns of argumentation is perhaps also facilitated by the fact that their structure is very close to categorical syllogisms, which, as van Eemeren et al. (1997:210) argue, aim for a rational ideal and apply universally regardless of content. The rationality and universality of these patterns render them more easily transferable cross-linguistically, at least more so than rhetorical patterns shaped by sociocultural traditions peculiar to the speech community of their origin.

2. Studies of interlingual influences in language contact situations traditionally use "financial" metaphors such as borrowing, loan words, or transfer. Since here we are dealing with the borrowing of a whole, self-contained rhetorical system, the medical metaphor of "transplant" is perhaps quite appropriate. By extension, one may consider, for example, the risk of "rejection" of the new system by the "recipient" rhetorical tradition.

sociopolitical power wielded by elites imbued with Western culture and education that precipitated the adoption of French discursive conventions. The latter were probably seen as "prestigious discourse" (Hyland 2000:175) better suited for handling complex socioeconomic relations necessary for the modernization of the country.

Second, the successful incorporation of French rhetorical patterns into Arabic discourse is quite remarkable in that rhetorical mixing is often frowned upon or outright rejected. Indeed, studies of contrastive rhetoric and academic discourse (Pennycook 1994; Connor 1996; Hyland 2000) indicate that discourse communities often resist the introduction of external rhetorical conventions into their genres. For example, nonnative speakers who wish to publish in English are often strongly advised to have their submissions checked by native speakers in order to rid them of linguistic and rhetorical interferences from the authors' first languages (Hyland 2000:174). Flowerdew (2000) documents the case of "Oliver," a Chinese scholar who submitted an article to an English journal only to see it completely changed through the editorial process. "Entire paragraphs were removed, and virtually every sentence rewritten" by the in-house editor, "who changed not only surface stylistic features but also . . . the whole organization of the manuscript." This led Oliver to believe that the editor reshaped the focus of the submission, "putting his own agenda on the paper" (Flowerdew 2000:139–42). As suggested earlier, the success of the transfer of French rhetoric into Arabic can be attributed, at least partially, to the familiarity of the law professionals involved with the rhetoric of both Arabic and French. In other words, this bi-rhetorical expertise, so to speak, has led to more tolerance of external rhetorical conventions, subsequently adopted and maintained, albeit with some adjustments. A possible implication of this is that discourse communities who are keen on protecting the "purity" of their rhetorical conventions may need to reconsider their position and avoid the exclusion of scholars with different rhetoric and epistemological backgrounds, who otherwise would enrich and diversify these discourse communities not only through the substance of their contribution, but also through their novel intellectual styles.

2. CONSEQUENCES OF BORROWING ON THE HOST LANGUAGE

The wholesale borrowing of rhetorical patterns raises an important question: What are the linguistic and discursive consequences of incorporating items of the magnitude described above into their host rhetorical tradition? First, in order to develop an idea of the type of linguistic consequences involved, I describe two salient morphosyntactic adjustments in the Arabic judgments that accommodate the transfer of the French rhetorical patterns before addressing the crucial question of how the rhetorical borrowing has an impact on the discourse of the host language.

2.1. Morphosyntactic Adjustments

The first adjustment concerns the use of the topicalization particle *'inna* at the beginning of court judgments. Earlier Moroccan Supreme Court judgments[3] replicated closely the syntax of the French judgments where the subject is separated from the predicate because of embedding. The judgment begins with the noun phrase subject *La Cour* "the court" followed by intervening dependent clauses that contain the different arguments, while the predicate, which states the verdict, is relegated to the end of the judgment as shown in (1), which summarizes the structure of the French judgment included in Appendix C.

(1)	La Cour . . .	The Court . . .
	Attendu que . . .	Considering that . . .
	Attendu que . . .	Considering that . . .
	Attendu que . . .	Considering that . . .
	Mais attendu que . . .	But considering that . . .
	Par ces motifs rejette . . .	For these reasons rejects . . .

Notice that the subject NP, *La Cour* "The Court" and the predicate *rejette* . . . "rejects . . ." are separated by several clauses that outline steps in the court's argumentation. The Arabic version, though, instead of using only the noun phrase *almajlis* "the court" in sentence-initial position as in French, adds the topicalization particle *'inna* as shown the following structure of an earlier court judgment.

(2)	'inna almajlis	[Particle]The Court
	Haythu 'anna . . .	Considering that . . .
	Haythu . . .	Considering . . .
	wa Haythu . . .	And considering . . .
	laakin Haythu . . .	But considering . . .
	wa Haythu 'anna . . .	And considering that . . .
	lihaadhihi al'asbaab	For these reasons
	qaDaa birafDi aTTalab	rules to reject the petition

(*majallat alqaDaa' wa alqaanuun*, 140–41, 1989:186–87)

3. See, for example, the Supreme Court Judgments in *Majallat alqaDaa' wa alqaanuun*, numbers 140 and 141, published by the Moroccan Ministry of Justice in 1989.

The addition of *'inna* seems to be motivated by the heavy multiple embedding; while in French such embedding is relatively unmarked, it is less so in Arabic, especially without the use of *'inna*. In other words, *'inna* enhances the acceptability of this type of subordination. Consider the semantically equivalent sentences in (3) and (4).

(3) Le professeur, après qu'il eut donné une conférence très intéressante sur le langage juridique, est reparti à Londres.

(4) al'ustaadhu ba'da 'an 'alqaa muHaaDaratan mufiidatan jiddan Hawla lughati alqaanuun raja'a 'ilaa landan.
The professor, after he had given a very interesting lecture on legal language, returned to London.

While in both Arabic and French the least marked option is the simple juxtaposition of the main clause and the subordinate clause (instead of embedding), the French structure (3) sounds less marked than its Arabic equivalent (4). On the basis of my own grammaticality judgment, the addition of the topicalization particle *'inna* before *al'ustaad* "the professor" makes sentence (4) far more acceptable. Even so, the lengthy separation of the subject and the predicate in the Arabic judgments remains contrived, which probably explains why this practice has been dropped in more recent court judgments: now the dependent clauses precede the main clause, which contains both subject and predicate, yielding the syntactic pattern illustrated in (5), where the main clause is in italics.

(5)	Haythu 'anna . . .	Considering that . . .
	Haythu 'anna . . .	Considering that . . .
	Haythu 'anna . . .	Considering that . . .
	qarraraa lmajlis . . .	*the court rules . . .*

A second adjustment concerns the nomination of topics that the court decides to address. The French judgments often use the simple and concise formula *sur X,* literally "on X" meaning "concerning X . . ." (e.g., *sur le premier moyen* "concerning the first ground" or *sur la recevabilité* "concerning admissibility"; cf. Cornu 1990:345). The Arabic judgments, on the other hand, resort to the more periphrastic expression *fiimaa yata'allaqu bi X . . .* "in what concerns X . . ." The latter is often modified, presumably to achieve stylistic variation and avoid monotony. Other substitutions include expressions such as *fiimaa yaxuSSu X . . . , fiimaa yarji'u 'ilaa X . . . , fiimaa yashmalu X . . .* , which are equivalent in meaning to "concerning X . . ." Thus, although the French and the Arabic devices for topic nomination are functionally similar, they differ in the degree of formulaicity, so to speak: in the Arabic phrases the syntactic pattern is fixed; but the lexical content, namely the verb, is allowed to vary.

These adjustments are not surprising and are indeed consistent with patterns that have been observed in the literature on lexical borrowing, for example. Borrowed words are often modified to fit the phonology or the morphology of the host language. For instance, the French word *pompe* "pump" is borrowed into Moroccan Arabic (MA) as *bumba,* where the sound [b] is used instead of the original French [p] because MA does not have the voiceless bilabial stop. Sometimes borrowed nouns are assigned a different grammatical gender. The French word *sacoche* "bag," which is feminine, is used in MA as a masculine noun, probably because it lacks the typical Arabic feminine ending "-a." Furthermore, these adjustments seem to follow general theories of transfer developed in other fields such as educational psychology and writing, where items learned in a particular domain are not simply reused in new and unfamiliar contexts but are reshaped to accommodate properties of these novel contexts. DePalma and Ringer (2011) use the term *adaptive transfer* to describe this phenomenon in the field of second language writing.

2.2. Impact of the Transfer of French Patterns on Arabic Rhetoric

The attested transfer into Arabic of an entire set of French rhetorical patterns affects the rhetoric of the host language in important ways and necessitates a reconceptualization of some of its aspects. A first consequence of this transfer is that the juxtaposition of new rhetorical features from French and indigenous ones naturally leads to more variation in Arabic generic features. This is, for example, the case of structures used to cite previous texts. The modes of citing the Quran and hadith in the fatwas have been developed within the Arabic rhetorical tradition and, over the centuries, have retained much of their formal properties, as suggested by the striking similarities between a citation from a medieval fatwa in (6) by the fourteenth-century mufti Ibn Taymiyya and a citation from a contemporary fatwa in (7). In both examples, the reporting clause ("In Muslim's sound collection . . . said") is exactly the same.

(6) fii SaHiihi muslim ʿan ʾabii hurayra raDiya allaahu ʿanhu ʿani annabiyyi Sallaa allaahu ʿalayhi wa sallam ʾannahu qaal: "almuʾminu alqawiyyu xayrun wa ʾaHabbu ʾilaa allaah . . ."
In Muslim's sound collection according to Abii Hurayra [honorific expression], the prophet [honorific expression] said: "God prefers strong believers . . ."

(Ibn Taymiyya 2002, 1:108)

(7) fii SaHiihi muslim 'an 'abii hurayra raDiya allaahu 'anhu 'ani annabiyyi Sallaa allaahu 'alayhi wa sallam 'annahu qaal: "juzzuu ashshawaarib . . ." In Muslim's sound collection according to Abii Hurayra [honorific expression] the prophet [honorific expression] said: "trim your moustaches . . ."

(Rifaa'ii 1988, 3:315)

The court judgments, on the other hand, adopt modes of citation borrowed from French, as demonstrated by the striking similarities between (8) and (9). These modes are obviously at variance with the traditional citations found in fatwas.

(8) a. binaa'an 'alaa alfaSl 345 min qaanuuni almisTarati almadaniyya . . .
According to article 345 of the code of civil procedure . . .

(*Al Milaf* 2005, 5:255)

b. 'amalan bimuqtaDayaati alfaSl 929 min qaanuuni al'iltizaamaati wa al'uquud . . .
In application of the stipulations of article 929 of the code of obligations and contracts . . .

(Supreme Court 2006, 64–65:22)

(9) a. Vu l'article 1382 du code civil . . .
Considering article 1382 of the civil code . . .

(Cour de Cassation, Decision 68-10.276, February 27, 1970)

b. En application des articles R. 142-1 et R. 142-18 du code de la sécurité sociale . . .
In application of articles R 142-1 and R 142-18 of the code of Social Security . . .

(Cour de Cassation, Decision 03948, December 2002)

The point made here is that the retention of old traditional modes of citing previous texts coupled with the introduction of new ones has now given rise to synchronic variation in modes of citation in Arabic. A similar point can be made regarding the frequency of nominalization in Arabic discourse. Like the French judgments,[4] the Arabic court judgments exhibit a high frequency of nominalization, which does not seem

4. Preference for nominalization in French court judgments is illustrated by the following example, where the content of the nominal expression (given in boldface) could have been as easily rendered by a tensed clause such as "*(before) they have received the registered letter from the court clerk's office.*"

"Qu'en statuant ainsi, alors qu'aucune diligence n'incombait aux parties avant **la réception de la lettre recommandée du greffe** . . . , la cour d'appel a violé les textes susvisés."

to be the case in the fatwas (see earlier discussion in chapter 4). However, further quantitative analysis is needed, using data from different genres (e.g., media and academic writing) in order to develop a more accurate idea of the variation in the frequency of nominalization across Arabic text types and to identify reliable accounts of the phenomenon.

A second consequence of borrowing French rhetoric is the need to revise the taxonomy of Arabic legal genres to include the court judgments based on the French model, with its specific rhetorical organization. The following diagram may be proposed as a partial representation of legal genres.

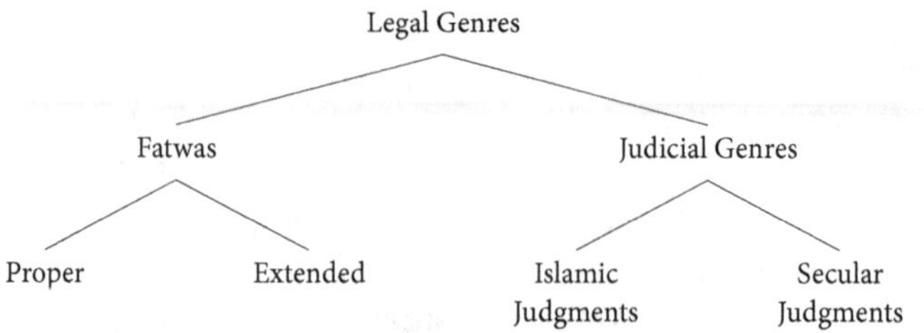

The traditional indigenous genres are proper fatwas with a limited answer-support format, extended fatwas that go beyond this format and include advice and exhortations, for example, and Islamic judgments rendered by *sharii'a* courts. The secular judgments include those with rhetorical patterns borrowed from French judicial discourse.

The third and perhaps most important consequence of the transfer of French patterns in the Arabic court judgments concerns the necessity to provide a reconceptualization of Arabic argumentation. Koch (1983) and Hatim (1997) present fundamental characterizations of Arabic arguments that can serve as a useful basis for such reconceptualization. According to Koch (1983), features of Arabic prose such as repetition, paraphrase, and balanced parallelism are the preferred modes of constructing arguments, in addition to their important role in achieving textual cohesion. The author draws a distinction between situations where logical argumentation is necessary to establish the truth because of the existence of doubt and uncertainty and situations where the truths are clear and accepted

---

"By so ruling, whereas no diligence rests with the parties before **the reception of the registered letter from the court clerk's office . . .** , the court of appeals violated the above mentioned texts."

(*Cour de Cassation*, Decision 07-22.074, January 15, 2009)

"in the particular universe of discourse" (Koch 1983:53). In the latter case, the argumentation consists simply in pointing out the truth and making it available to the audience through *presentation.* The author suggests that presentation is the dominant mode of persuasion in Arabic and describes it the following terms:

> An arguer presents his truths by making them present in discourse: by repeating them, paraphrasing them, doubling them, calling attention to them with external particles. (Koch 1983:55)

Data from the present study appear to bear out this view of argumentation. As mentioned earlier, muftis often support their opinions by citing hadith. It is sometimes the case that the mufti presents several versions of the hadith with essentially the same content. In Qaradawi (1981:529–30) the mufti indicates that employment in banks that engage in interest-based transactions is prohibited because of a hadith and then proceeds to repeat its content in the following three versions:

(10) a. la'ana 'aakila arribaa wa mu'akkilahu wa shaahidayhi.
[the prophet] curses the usury receiver, the usury provider, and the witnesses to such transaction.
b. la'ana 'aakila arribaa wa mu'akkilahu wa shaahidayhi wa kaatibahu.
[the prophet] curses the usury receiver, the usury provider, the witnesses to such transaction, and its drafter.
c. 'aakilu arribaa wa mu'akkiluhu wa shaahidaahu . . . mal'uunuun.
The usury receiver, the usury provider, and the witnesses to such transaction . . . are all cursed.

In the "universe of discourse" of fatwas, to borrow Koch's phrase, the mere presentation of a hadith (or a verse from the Quran) is deemed sufficient to persuade believers of the validity of a particular claim. The argumentation may be strengthened through "accumulating and insisting" (Johnstone 1991:93), as in (a) through (c) above.

For his part, Hatim (1997:39–40) distinguishes two types of argumentation: *through-argumentation* and *counter-argumentation.* The first type consists in presenting a single point of view and substantiating it. The second type, counter-argumentation, "is initiated by a selective summary of someone else's viewpoint, followed by a counter-claim, a substantiation outlining the grounds for the opposition, and finally a conclusion." The author suggests that while Arabic exhibits evidence of counter-argumentation, it tends to favor through-argumentation. Both types of argumentation are used in fatwas. Through-argumentation is used in a fatwa mentioned earlier where the mufti declares that work in banks that engage in interest-based transactions is not permissible because the Quran and hadith prohibit usurious activities (Ibn Baz in Rifaa'ii 1988, 2:280). Another fatwa that deals with the same issue uses counter-argumentation. The mufti acknowledges the prohibition of usurious activities, but introduces a different view based on the principle of *aDDaruura* "necessity" and states that employment in banks is permissible, since interest-based transactions are unavoidable in today's world of finance (Qaradawi 1981:529). The solution proposed in this second fatwa is reminiscent of the *argumentum a coherentia* (Feteris1999:54–55) used in Western legal systems to resolve conflicts between legal rules, preferring for example the application of a new rule rather than an old one. In order to support his opinion, the mufti chose the principle of *aDDaruura,* which is sometimes used to avoid severe consequences of the strict application of *sharii'a* law.

With the borrowing of French patterns in Arabic court judgments, Arabic discourse has clearly acquired an additional type of argumentation (see earlier discussion of this issue in chapter 3). What is more crucial, though, is that, compared with the indigenous types outlined above (presentation, through-argumentation, and counter-argumentation), the borrowed mode of argumentation is qualitatively different in that it is more complex and requires more elaborate rhetorical and linguistic manipulations. In fact, as previous analyses indicate, the argument structure in the court judgments is quite close to the structure of syllogisms, since it consists of a sequence of "premises" signaled by the expression *Haythu 'anna* . . . "considering that . . . ," which introduces the relevant points on which the decision is to be made. These premises logically lead to the conclusion of the court, its verdict, which is signaled by the phrase *lihaadhihi al'asbaab* "for these reasons . . ."

In order to accommodate the complexity resulting from the borrowing of rhetorical patterns, Arabic legal argumentation may now be characterized in terms of a formality continuum along which various types of arguments can be placed. The most formal type of argument, the quasi-syllogistic structure of the court judgment, is placed at one end of the continuum, and at the other end is the least formal type, simple presentation as conceived by Koch (1983). Hatim's through-argumentation and counter-argumentation occupy intermediate positions. The following figure recapitulates and illustrates the main components of the proposed continuum.

Most Formal Argumentation
Quasi-syllogistic argument: court judgments modeled on French patterns;
Counter-argumentation: fatwas with two viewpoints (Qaradawi 1981:529);
Through-argumentation: fatwas with a single viewpoint (Ibn Baz in Rifaa'ii 1988, 2:280);
Presentation and repetition "as proof": citations of hadith and Quran.
Least Formal Argumentation

The view of argumentation outlined above has several advantages. First, it provides a more complete picture of Arabic arguments and a classification based on formality that can easily accommodate other types of arguments. What is needed is further research that identifies other sites of argumentation (e.g., judgments by Islamic courts; see Fakhri 2002), analyzes the structure of the arguments they use, and determines where these may fit in the proposed continuum. Second, this conceptualization of Arabic argumentation is consistent with features of argumentation present in Western rhetoric, partially because of the borrowing involved. In Western rhetoric, formal argumentation based on traditional Aristotelian categorical syllogisms coexists with less formal types of argumentation advocated by contemporary rhetoricians and philosophers of language (e.g.,Toulmin 1958; Perelman and Olbrechts-Tyteca 1969) to account for common arguments designed to persuade audiences during regular social interaction. Thus, while syllogisms consist of a formal and presumably universal pattern that, regardless of subject matter, seeks to establish the truth of new statements (conclusions) on the basis of statements (premises) known to be true (van Eemeren et al. 1997), the Toulmin model is less formal and consists of a claim, supporting evidence (grounds), and a warrant that explicitly relates the grounds to the claim.

Third, the proposed model is intended to be dynamic in that it triggers questions regarding the selection among available types of arguments. The most determinant factor in the choice of an argument is probably the intended audience, a proposition supported by both Western and Arabic rhetorical traditions. For example, Perelman and Olbrechts-Tyteca (1969) consider that argumentation is always addressed to an audience and that its evaluation should be based on the extent to which it is accepted by the audience rather than solely on its formal validity (see Feteris 1999:48–49). The awareness of effect of audience on arguments is not absent in Arabic rhetoric. Hatim (1997:48) highlights the importance given to audience in the construction of arguments by early Arab rhetoricians such as al-Jurjaani, al-ʿAskari, and al-Sakkaaki. These rhetoricians consider that the formulation of arguments has to take into account the characteristics of the audience to which these arguments are addressed, especially the intensity of their opposition to the claims put forth. A different degree of evaluative discourse and emphasis is required, depending on whether the addressee is "one who denies" the claims made (*munkir*), one who is uncertain (*mutaraddid*), or one who is open-minded (*khaali al-dhihn*).

Another aspect of the dynamic nature of the proposed model is the potential "competition" among the different types of arguments and the eventual diachronic developments to which it may lead and which will alter the current configuration of the model. A particularly interesting issue worthy of attention is the possibility that over time the argumentation pattern borrowed from French into Arabic court judgments may encroach on the indigenous types of arguments and even spread to other genres within and outside the legal domain. This is not inconceivable given the constant fluctuation of genres and their tendency to overlap with each other. The potential spread of the borrowed type of argumentation and its frequency of use is likely to have an impact on Arabic thought patterns and lead to newly acquired intellectual styles in legal and academic discourse communities, a phenomenon reminiscent of the famous Sapir-Whorf hypothesis that language influences thought. The consideration of these possibilities should open novel and exciting areas of inquiry. In sum, the appeal of the proposed reconceptualization of Arabic argumentation lies in its completeness, its hints of universality as indicated by properties that it shares with Western rhetoric, its dynamic nature, and its capacity to generate further insights about Arabic discourse and Arabic discourse communities. The proposal is also congruent with postmodern cross-cultural views that reject the often simplistic and static construction of the rhetorical traditions of others (Kubota and Lehner 2004) in favor of highlighting the complexity and richness of these traditions.

3. FATWAS AND THEIR SOCIOCULTURAL MILIEU: MUTUAL INFLUENCES

In earlier analysis, the linguistic and rhetorical structures found in the fatwas have been accounted for in terms of particular contextual factors such as the characteristics of participants (knowledgeable and even erudite *muftis* versus lay *mustaftis* seeking guidance) or the purpose of the genre (providing a nonbinding opinion). These accounts are thus based on the "proximate" context, in other words, the immediate features of the communicative event (Phillips and Hardy 2002:19). Genre studies have shown that consideration of the broader sociocultural context, the "distal context," may also yield further insights about how genre tokens are shaped and how they influence their environment. For instance, Devitt (2004:26–27) underscores the notion that "contexts beyond the more immediate context of situation of a particular genre partially construct what genres are and are in turn constructed (reproduced) by people performing genre action." Thus in this section I will consider the broader sociocultural climate surrounding the issuing of fatwas, and show how it complements the proximate contextual factors and further enhances our understanding of the rhetoric of fatwas. First, I will briefly describe salient aspects of this sociocultural climate (section 3.1) before attempting to elucidate their impact on the rhetorical structure of fatwas (section 3.2).

3.1. The Sociocultural Climate

The most salient and relevant property of the climate surrounding contemporary *'iftaa'* is the revival of Islamic values and the emergence of political and civic entities with Islamic leanings and ideologies. There is a vast literature on this topic, and it is beyond the scope of the present study to discuss it in a detailed and comprehensive manner. The discussion will, therefore, be limited to a broad outline of some of the main ideas on the subject, including the increasing attention to Islamic traditions and the subsequent tension between these and Western influences.

The role of Islam has always been preeminent in Arab communities even during the period where there were attempts to build secular nation-states inspired by nationalist or socialist ideologies in the Arab world. The failure of those attempts in the second half of the twentieth century has emboldened political Islam and led to greater infusion of religion into the sphere of politics (Tibi 2001:3). This change has been facilitated in many instances by the fact that seemingly secular states did not respond adequately to the socioeconomic needs and aspirations of the Arab-Muslim communities. Furthermore, secularism was in many instances seen as an ideology imported from the West by Western-educated elites and did not particularly appeal to society at large. Consequently, large segments of Muslim communities rejected it in favor of political Islam, as an alternative to deal with social and economic difficulties. The renewed prominence of religious values in different aspects of social life has led to the multiplicity of different religious actors, parties, and organizations. Ultimately, recent events of the so-called Arab spring enabled Islamist parties to gain power in several Arab countries such as Egypt, Tunisia, and to some extent Morocco.[5]

However, as Tibi (2001:6–7) cogently argues, political Islam has not rejected Western culture as a whole, but has sought "to adapt modernity instrumentally" by keeping and utilizing its material achievements. The author uses the term "Islamic dream of semi-modernity" to capture Islamists' willingness to adopt modern scientific and technological tools while at the same time rejecting the worldview and the value systems that underlie their development. The continuous, albeit sometimes resented, presence in Muslim communities of aspects of Western culture constitutes a significant challenge to large segments of these communities, as described by Roy (2004:154) in the following excerpt:

> True believers are confronted with ways of life, images, films, cultural models, educational systems, consumer habits and economic practices that are heavily influenced by a secular western world.

The competing Western and Islamic traditions and ideologies create an environment filled with tension, uncertainty, and turmoil. The situation is further exacerbated by the emergence of a large number of freelance, self-proclaimed religious figures who operate at the periphery of religious centers of authority (e.g., Al-Azhar in Egypt) and by the proliferation of businesses and charities with Islamic leanings that thrive outside the system of official state-sanctioned socioeconomic entities (Roy 2004:117–75).[6]

---

5. The Islamist parties in Egypt and Tunisia have succeeded in taking charge as the principle governing bodies, but recent events show that the political situation in both countries is far from stable: Tunisia has seen quite a bit of violence, especially attacks against secular militants, and in Egypt the Islamist president has been removed by the army, which has triggered large protests and a great deal of violence. The situation in Morocco is quite different. The Moroccan Islamist party, the Party of Justice and Development, has been designated by the king to form a government pursuant to its obtaining more votes in the legislative elections than any of its competitors. In spite of economic difficulties and the withdrawal of the Istiqlal Party from the governing coalition, the political situation in Morocco appears to be relatively stable.

6. A whole "industry" seems to have developed around many of these religious activists that disseminate their ideas and opinions on a multitude of religious and social topics through appearances on radio and TV shows and through the sale of books, cassette tapes, videos, and CDs that contain their lectures and sermons. In major cities in the Arab world, one can easily obtain these products in various specialized distribution points or simply through ubiquitous vendors in street corners.

The tension-filled environment described affects the institution of *'iftaa'* and muftis and fatwa seekers. Muftis themselves contribute to the social tensions, since their fatwas are often controversial and draw a great deal of criticism, bringing to the surface conflicts between traditional values and more progressive ones. Fatwas are regularly criticized and even strongly opposed by members of the *'iftaa'* community themselves, whether individual muftis or mufti councils. For example, a fatwa allowing the marriage of girls as young as nine has been fiercely contested by the Moroccan *Superior Council of 'ulamaa'*, which portrayed the author of the fatwa as "*une personne connue pour ses tendances à la subversion et à l'amalgame autour des constantes de la Oumma et de son rite*" [a person known for his leanings toward subversion and confusion regarding the permanent features of the Muslim community and its rite] (*Aujourd'hui Le Maroc,* September 22, 2008).[7] Fatwas have also been criticized by entities outside the institution of *'iftaa'*. This happens frequently in the media, which often point out the topical irrelevance of many fatwas. For example, the popular commentator Rachid Nini, who was formerly associated with the Moroccan daily *almasaa'*, has criticized muftis for their excessive preoccupation with what he considers trivial issues such as the question of shopping in supermarkets that sell alcohol, instead of focusing on major social and governance problems such as the accountability of public officials.[8]

Conclusions and Implications

Fatwa seekers are also affected, since social discord tends to create uncertainty and confusions and individuals are forced to make important difficult choices. Resorting to muftis is therefore an obvious way for many believers to find answers to questions that concern them. Indication of fatwa seekers' predicaments can be found, for example, in fatwas that have dealt with the issue of employment in banks that practice interest-based transactions. Although many Muslim countries do not prohibit work in such institutions, citizens of those countries still feel the need to be assured regarding the position of *sharii'a* on this issue and the appropriate conduct to adopt. Matters are further complicated by the ubiquity of modern banks in Muslim communities and the need for their services,

7. According to the Moroccan daily *Aujourd'hui Le Maroc* of September 23, 2008, the courts even opened an investigation concerning this fatwa. It should be noted that Article 19 of the Moroccan Family Code (*Moudawwana*) establishes the age of marriage for both males and females at 18.

8. In the December 12, 2009, issue of *almasaa'*, Nini writes the following:

> Instead of issuing fatwas about the prohibition of shopping in department stores that sell alcohol . . . , our honorable religious scholars should issue fatwas regarding those representatives that leave their parliament seats empty and refuse to discuss the budget bill which affects the fate of thirty-three million Moroccans. . . .

which creates uncertainty even for muftis and leads them to divergent opinions. As discussed earlier, while some muftis prohibit employment in modern banks on the basis of verses from the Quran concerning *ribaa* "usury," others allow it under the theory of *aDDaruura* "necessity."

3.2. Impact on the Rhetoric of Fatwas

The following discussion attempts to show how elements of the broader sociocultural environment strengthen the "proximate context" accounts provided earlier for fatwa rhetoric and points to possible changes in the fatwa as a genre. Given the prevailing contentious sociocultural environment described, muftis take advantage of requests for information about *sharii'a* issues to shore up their social status and strive to retain their relevance and legitimacy. These goals are achieved through rhetorical constructions introduced in the fatwas. The judicious rhetorical choices concerning the modes of citations where elaborate references to the prophet, his companions, and other highly regarded hadith transmitters serve not simply as objective means for establishing the authenticity of hadith, but also to impress fatwa seekers by displaying muftis' detailed knowledge of *sharii'a* matters (see discussion in chapter 3). Furthermore, the expansion of fatwa moves beyond the obligatory answer-support format to include advice and moral guidance portrays the mufti as a thoughtful, caring figure who is concerned about the spiritual needs of questioners striving in an uncertain and precarious social order. Other rhetorical devices such as the use of rhetorical softeners and hedges (see example [17] in chapter 3) are designed to moderate potentially controversial opinions and reflect the contentiousness of the prevailing circumstances where muftis need to be cautious and mindful of potential negative reactions to their fatwas from various social constituencies with different views and agendas.

These rhetorical patterns, which indicate muftis' endeavor to remain relevant and attentive to their environment and audience, constitute innovations that surpass the specific purpose of the fatwa, namely answering questions about *sharii'a*. It is clear, for example, that the frequent addition in fatwas of evaluative moves such as advice and lament violates traditional charges to muftis to be concise and avoid speculation, and even to refrain from issuing fatwas altogether in case of uncertainty (see discussion of *'adab almufti* "mufti conduct" in chapter 2). However, these innovations that serve muftis' agendas are not surprising. First, they are consistent with findings about genres and their evolution. Innovations are often introduced by members of particular discourse communities with highest expertise in content and rhetoric who "exploit the rules and conventions of a genre in order to achieve special effects or private intentions, as it were . . ." (Bhatia 1993:14). Indeed, the rhetoric of fatwas seems to support this view in that it is often renowned and well-established muftis such as Sheikh Qaradawi who tend to issue elaborate fatwas with multiple moves designed to give advice or explanations, for example. Second, these innovations in the rhetoric of fatwas are facilitated by shifts in the kind of topics addressed. As discussed in chapter 2, Muslim communities nowadays, in spite of the resistance of entities with Islamic leanings, have adopted secular laws that regulate "technical" aspects of everyday social and economic activity. Consequently, the topical scope of contemporary fatwas is increasingly reduced to broader issues involving basic and somewhat moralistic questions about what is permissible and what is not, questions that call for answers based on general precepts drawn from the Quran and hadith (e.g., "the cooperation on sin and transgression" or the theory of *aDDaruura* "necessity" discussed earlier). The broader moral nature of these issues is likely to trigger evaluative moves involving advice and moral guidance.[9] In sum, given the cumulative effects of "proximate" and "distal" contextual factors and the change in topical focus, rhetorical innovations by muftis appear to be a natural development of the fatwa genre.

These rhetorical changes have important consequences for fatwas as a genre because they alter the role relations between muftis and the fatwa recipients. The latter are now put in the position of students and advisees with educational and spiritual needs, in addition to their status as *mustaftis* seeking answers to questions about *sharii'a*. This shift in role relations in turn changes the communicative purpose of the fatwa, a fundamental component of the definition of genre as discussed earlier, and blurs the distinction between fatwas and other genres, since now the purpose of fatwas, especially extended ones, overlaps with that of religious lectures and sermons. All these genres include explanation of *sharii'a* concepts, advice, and moral guidance and share the linguistic and rhetorical realizations entailed by these functions. These observations may raise questions regarding the validity of the name of the fatwa genre itself because now fatwas encompass tokens with varied purposes and textual properties. The reevaluation of genre labeling is legitimate especially if the labels are constructed by the discourse community that uses them. As suggested by Swales (1990:58), genre names need to be scrutinized to assess their validity:

9. Collections of ancient fatwas often discuss "technical" issues such as the following that appear in Al-Wanshariisii's *al-Mi'yaar* (Al-Wanshariisii 1981, V): Does rain water gathered in a rented house belong to the landlord or to the tenant? Or can one sell a house, but exclude from the sale the vineyard inside it? Nowadays disputes involving matters such as these are likely to be resolved on the basis of secular regulations, codes, or statutes.

> The genre names inherited and produced by discourse communities and imported by others constitute valuable ethnographic communication, *but typically need further validation.* (my emphasis)

The important issues raised by this exploratory discussion warrant further investigations, which may be challenging, but which will no doubt yield important insights, especially if one selects appropriate theoretical approaches among the promising ones now available. In this respect, Bhatia's (2008) *critical genre analysis* is particularly suitable as a theoretical framework. Critical genre analysis investigates how linguistic and rhetorical patterns in a particular genre may be used to promote certain ideologies that often produce and maintain social inequalities. As Devitt (2004:12) suggests, genre manipulation and alteration are quite often used to mislead audiences. She mentions, for example, how a mundane genre such as sales letters may be disguised as official government correspondence, a very different genre, in order to lure potential customers to read about the products that the letters are designed to promote.

Critical genre analysis will enable researchers to investigate how muftis, especially influential ones, may use their rhetorical skills to alter the purpose of fatwas in important ways so as to promote particular viewpoints and ideologies. This is all the more important given that the occasion of fatwa issuing often affords them lay questioners as captive audiences that can be easily manipulated. Particularly vulnerable to such manipulation are women and other community members with low levels of education and literacy rates. The goal here is not to systematically attribute inappropriate motives to muftis; it is rather to highlight the importance of understanding the role of this genre and its potential use as a tool to influence behaviors, beliefs, and value systems under the guise of simply informing community members about *sharii'a* rules. It is legitimate therefore to resort to critical genre analysis in order to unravel cases where muftis exceed their role as providers of information about *sharii'a.* For example, in a fatwa discussed earlier (see chapter 3 footnote 9), the mufti declares that *sharii'a* does not forbid a woman to include in her marriage contract stipulations that allow her to divorce her husband (Al-Ahmad 2003, 2:108). However, the mufti proceeds to discourage women from actually taking advantage of this right under the pretext that such stipulations may offend prospective husbands. Application of critical genre analysis in this instance will highlight inequalities between participants in this particular social transaction and show that unwarranted mufti excesses are simply reflections of biases against women. Indeed, the mufti could have chosen to empower women by addressing his advice to men instead and exhorting them to respect *sharii'a* precepts that allow women to introduce stipulations in their marriage contracts. This point is further developed below (see section 4.4 on gender and access to discourse).

4. REMARKS ON GENRE AND CULTURE

I pointed out earlier (see chapter 1, section 2) that given the traditional centrality of juridical sciences in Muslim culture and the vast scholarship that results from it, legal texts such as fatwas and court judgments have been a major source of sociocultural information about Arab and Muslim communities at various periods of their history (Lagardère 1995; Powers 2002; Al-Jabri 2003). Studies of the *content* of these texts have yielded information about social customs, family relations, and economic activities, and in general shed light on communal values and belief systems. Readers may glean similar cultural information from the content of excerpts and notes presented earlier; however, the focus of the following discussion is *not* on the *content* of the texts considered, but on the rhetorical patterns and generic practices involved in the production and use of the fatwas and court judgments and what these patterns and practices reveal about contemporary Arab communities. The discussion builds upon debates concerning various cultural traits and temperaments that have been presented in previous research, particularly in studies from the field of contrastive rhetoric and genre analysis (Connor 1996; Hatim 1997; Fakhri 2004). An important note of caution needs to be made from the outset in order to avoid any impression of stereotyping or cultural reduction. The various statements about cultural features are not claimed to be applicable across the board to all social entities, groupings, or academic disciplines. They represent possible interpretations and implications of the generic practices identified in the present data analysis. Four main points are made which concern intellectual styles, politeness and face, utilitarian comportments, and gender and access to discourse.

4.1. Intellectual Styles: Thought Clarity and Explicitness

Hatim (1997:161) notes with dismay the "pronouncements often made regarding the so-called 'mentality' of the Arabs" in the following terms:

> Arabic, we are told, is characterized by a general vagueness of thought which stems from over-emphasis on the symbol at the expense of its meaning.

The author argues that such conclusions are unwarranted and "practically meaningless." He shows that rhetorical features such as persuasion by simple presentation and ubiquitous figurative language and hyperbole, which are often cited as characteristics of Arabic prose, are not peculiar to Arabic. The author provides English examples of "argumentation by presentation" and invites the reader to "browse through any issues of Hansard (the verbatim record of the British parliament) for interesting examples of extended metaphors" (Hatim 1997:164). The analysis in the present study is congruent with Hatim's position in that it further shows that while the fatwas include argumentation by presentation, the syllogistic model of argumentation found in the court judgments is clearly not indicative of "a general vagueness of thought." The rhetoric of Arabic argumentation described above exhibits a great deal of complexity and hybridity, with the court judgments relying on tightly structured logical organization and the fatwas exhibiting instances of ethos and affective appeal. However, this refutation of "vagueness of thought" may not be as strong in domains other than law. Data from humanities academic discourse presented in Fakhri (2004:1129) suggest at least a degree of "intellectual casualness." For example, one of the authors quoted in that study enumerates seven groups of thinkers with different views about Arab unity, but fails to identify precisely who these thinkers are or in what academic fora they have expressed those views. Such a lapse is particularly grave in academic writing.

The issue of directness or explicitness as a rhetorical feature has also attracted a lot of attention partly because it is highly variable cross-culturally. Perhaps one of the best known framings of this issue is Hinds's (1987) proposal that distinguishes reader-responsible and writer-responsible rhetoric, represented respectively by Japanese and English traditions. In the former, the reader bears the burden of making sense of the text, while in the latter it is the responsibility of the writer to be clear and explicit and to facilitate reader comprehension through a direct statement of how the text is structured, for example. Fakhri (2004:1131) discusses the issue of explicitness in Arabic academic discourse and concludes that the latter does not fit neatly in either of Hinds's categories but is rather mixed, with authors showing different degrees of explicitness. Ideally, in the domain of law, explicitness has to be extremely valued: it is necessary for legal discourse to be direct and explicit in order to achieve justice, order, and peace. The court judgments considered are highly structured into a fixed rhetorical pattern that leaves little doubt regarding the intent of the court and the interpretation of its opinion. A court judgment may not be valid or acceptable to some, but it has to reflect clearly and unequivocally the position of the court. The assessment of explicitness in fatwas is a bit more problematic and needs to be nuanced. As discussed earlier, the main purpose of fatwas is to declare whether a particular conduct or activity is permissible under *sharii'a* rules. This clear-cut objective is sometimes blurred by additional commentary on the part of muftis, which makes otherwise clear *sharii'a* positions open to interpretation. For example, in one of the fatwas mentioned before, the mufti states that *sharii'a* does not prohibit women's work outside the home, but then he enumerates several constraints and conditions regarding the way female employees should conduct themselves in public that for some at least may cast doubt on the wisdom of seeking employment in the first place. In other words, the recipient of the fatwa has the responsibility of evaluating its content, including muftis' speculations, and deciding for herself the proper course of action to take. In contrast to this type of fatwa ambiguity, which results from the juxtaposition of *sharii'a* rules and muftis' personal commentary, the rhetoric of fatwas sometimes exhibits patterns that are more reader-friendly, such as instances where the mufti defines unfamiliar terms or explains legal concepts and principles. However, this pedagogical dimension is not necessarily devoid of self-interest on the part of the mufti, who may be more motivated by the concern to show off his erudition.

4.2. Politeness and Face

Studies on the rhetoric of different academic traditions often note the reluctance of authors to engage in aggressive critical evaluation of the work of others and the promotion of their own, presumably because such practices are face-threatening and therefore are stigmatized and deemed culturally inappropriate (Taylor and Chen 1991; Jogthong 2001). For example, it has been suggested that in the Chinese culture critical stances are at odds with Confucian values of honor and pride and need to be curtailed (Loi and Sweetnam Evans 2010:2819). Fakhri (2004:1129) addresses this issue in a study of a sample of Arabic research article introductions and reaches the following conclusion:

> While there are instances in [that] study where authors not only avoid criticism of others' scholarship but even explicitly admit the modesty of their research and its limitations, many authors are very assertive and do not shy away from expressing the importance of their contributions.

In principle, legal genres such as court judgments should not be expected to exhibit sentiments of humility and face-saving strategies given the adversarial nature of judicial proceedings: litigants and their representatives as well as judges are prone to be assertive and often confrontational. As earlier analysis indicates, the court judgments include unambiguously opinionated and forceful declarations, often using emphatic language peppered with hyperbole and exaggerations. The rhetoric of fatwas has been shown to contain instances of rather soft affective appeal, which is unavoidable when quoting from the Quran and hadith. However, as has also been demonstrated, muftis display a great deal of boldness and audacity by exceeding their role as purveyors of knowledge about *sharii'a* positions on specific questions of concern to fatwa seekers and engaging in unsolicited advice, exhortation, and even blame. The use of the phrase *wa allahu a'lam* "and God knows best" by some muftis may connote a measure of humility on their part; however, its apparent automatic use at the end of the fatwa indicates that it mostly serves a textual function, namely as a coda. At any rate, its occurrence in some fatwas is not sufficient to counterbalance the effect on readers of frequent audacious proclamations by muftis.

4.3. Utilitarian Comportments

The generic practices described in the study suggest utilitarian comportments on the part of the discourse communities involved. Thus, instead of clinging to the "purity" of Arabic legal rhetoric, as is the usual case of discourse communities keen on protecting their distinctive character, the Moroccan law professionals adopted French rhetorical patterns in the court judgments as a practical linguistic apparatus for dealing efficiently with the complex socioeconomic reality resulting from the desire to modernize their society. This is in a way the symbolic equivalent of the pragmatic adoption of Western technologies in Arab and Muslim communities in spite of lingering suspicions toward the West and its values in many quarters.

The proliferation of fatwas coupled with their nonbinding nature allows fatwa seekers to engage in what some have termed "fatwa shopping" and to search for friendly opinions that suit their purposes rather than strive for some elusive "truth" (Harding 2009). Haddad (1996) describes the "war of fatwas" that took place after the 1990 Iraq invasion of Kuwait and the U.S. intervention. Various Arab governments with opposite political agendas regarding whether to cooperate or not with Western forces against another Muslim country managed to secure fatwas that supported their position and protected their interests. The same utilitarian conduct is shown by private citizens who desire to engage in activities allowed by the secular laws of the communities where they reside and who, nevertheless, feel the need to seek the blessing of a willing mufti who approves of such activities. This is clearly the case of large numbers of Muslims who have migrated to Western Europe. For example, fatwas issued by Al-Moumni (1998) in

Rotterdam, Holland, suggest that fatwa seekers experience a great deal of apprehension regarding their new life in progressive host countries and particularly regarding how to interact with local populations that possess different values and lifestyles. In this instance, "fatwa shopping" is a means of obtaining spiritual comfort and peace of mind, since the new environment allows greater freedoms and more choices regarding conduct and lifestyle. In sum, contrary to the often negative impressions given by well-publicized and sensationalized fatwas, the institution of *'iftaa'* appears to have a useful role. Fatwas are an important tool for "social action," to use Carolyn Miller's term, that serves to guide believers through different ideological currents, secular and religious, and to reconcile traditional Islamic values and contemporary realities. In the words of a mufti interviewed in Farquhar (2009), fatwas serve to "close the gap between what the religion demands and what actually occurs."

4.4. Gender and Access to Discourse

A United Nations report on the state of women in the Arab world (UN Development Fund for Women 2004:18) notes that in spite of some advances, there are many factors that still hinder the realization of gender equality in the Arab countries and that many in these countries still perceive "gender equality as a western imposition that is inappropriate to the religious and cultural context of Arab states." It is obvious that a general discussion of the topic is beyond the scope of the present work, although the content of the fatwas and the court judgments may include relevant information about gender relations; however, it is legitimate to consider specifically what the generic practices described reveal about the issue of gender. The most obvious and particularly egregious manifestation of gender inequality can be framed in terms of women's lack of access to discourse. Van Dijk (1996:85–86) highlights the importance of the relationship between access to discourse and social power in the following terms:

> One major element in the discursive reproduction of power and dominance is the very *access* to discourse and communicative events. In this respect discourse is similar to other valued social resources that form the basis of power to which there is unequally distributed access. For instance, not everyone has equal access to the media, legal, political, bureaucratic or scholarly text and talk. That is, we need to explore the implications of the complex question *Who may speak or write to whom, about what, when, and in what context. . . .*

The question then is: To what extent do women have access to the genres considered here, the court judgments and fatwas? It is clear that women may be passive recipients of such texts, and it is also clear that they do not participate equally in their production. While it is not uncommon in many Arab countries to encounter women judges, fatwa issuing is exclusively dominated by male muftis. The gender inequality regarding access to *'iftaa'* is particularly inauspicious, since, as has been amply demonstrated, issuing a fatwa does not simply involve providing objective information about *sharii'a* rules. Muftis often engage in expressing personal beliefs, providing unsolicited advice, and promoting or stigmatizing particular conduct or activities with which they do not agree. In other words, denying women discursive access in the domain of *'iftaa'* not only deprives the community of more valuable scholarship, it also excludes female perspectives that would otherwise enrich the culture and provide alternative solutions to its problems. In a fatwa discussed earlier on whether women can exercise a measure of control over family relations through contractual stipulations, the mufti acknowledges the permissibility of such arrangements under *sharii'a* law, but then proceeds to discourage women from resorting to these legitimate legal means that empower them. One might wonder whether a woman mufti would engage in a similar generic practice or, if she did, would give a similarly discouraging opinion.

5. SUGGESTIONS FOR FURTHER RESEARCH

The analysis and discussions presented in this study have raised questions that still need to be addressed in order to gain a better understanding of Arabic genres and to develop a more complete picture of the generic conventions and practices of different discourse communities. The following suggestions outline topics for further research that will fill in some of the remaining gaps. The suggestions are sorted into two sets of questions: a general category that deals with different genre and discourse issues (1.a–f) and a second category that specifically concerns fatwas (2.a–f).

1. (a) Will the rhetorical patterns borrowed from French spread to other genres and types of discourse, leading to important rhetorical developments?
   What factors (e.g., education, appeal of the new patterns as symbols of modernity and rationality, etc.) may play a role in determining the scope and rate of these developments?
   (b) What other discourse domains and genres (academic texts, legal discourse from different Arab countries, etc.) show rhetorical borrowing? How can such borrowing be accounted for?

(c) What other types of argumentative texts are there? What are their characteristics, and how do they fit in the proposed formality continuum?

(d) What other genre-specific linguistic features are there? How are they different from general grammar rules in terms of their formal properties, functions, and frequency of occurrence?

(e) What are the effects of the diglossic situation of Arabic and the language variation associated with it on the construction of genres and their comprehension?

(f) What kinds of genre features may benefit from quantitative analyses, and how? (e.g., type/token ratios of lexical items or phrases, measurements of syntactic complexity, and frequency of particular meta-discourse features).

2. (a) What linguistic and rhetorical differences are there between written fatwas and oral fatwas delivered through radio and television, for example? What language variety (e.g., MSA, a regional dialect, or mixture of both) do they use, and why?

(b) What is the effect on the construction of fatwas of topic variability (e.g.,"technical" issues regarding division of property versus broader questions about moral conduct)?

(c) What kind of linguistic and rhetorical changes have occurred in the fatwas over time? What factors have motivated these changes?

(d) How do fatwa seekers' characteristics (e.g., gender, age, education) affect muftis' responses in terms of their content and rhetoric?

(e) What types of ideologies are promoted by fatwas that are issued in Arabic-speaking communities? How are these ideologies constructed linguistically and rhetorically?

(f) Instead of freelance muftis or mufti councils controlled by political institutions, under what circumstances will muftis be able to constitute a more coherent and "modern" discourse community with clear requirements for membership, well-defined modes of communication, and standardized generic conventions? What are the consequences of this change for the institution of *'iftaa'* and its role in contemporary Muslim communities?

Undoubtedly, investigations of these issues are bound to pose important challenges, since their successful completion will require apt selection of theoretical frameworks, careful collection of data with particular attention to contextual factors, and rigorous analysis. Some of these investigations may require "insider" information given the different cultures and disciplines involved; however, this problem can be solved through collaboration among scholars from different communities with different types of expertise (e.g., linguists, rhetoricians, jurists, law practitioners, and muftis). At any rate, this type of research is necessary in order to gain better understanding of Arabic discursive and rhetorical practices and to gain cultural knowledge about the communities where these practices occur. Only through serious commitment to this line of research can we surpass the usual discussions of textual features of Arabic prose and achieve a higher explanatory analysis of discursive rhetorical properties of texts commensurable with the treatment of more commonly studied languages and rhetorical traditions.

SUMMARY

This chapter has explored some implications of the study for genre analysis and Arabic discourse, beginning with a discussion of the significance of wholesale borrowing of rhetorical patterns and its impact on Arabic, the host language. The transfer of French rhetorical patterns is seen as a successful endeavor requiring only a few linguistic adjustments. This is particularly remarkable given that rhetorical mixing is often resisted by discourse communities that insist on preserving and protecting the purity of their generic conventions. In the present case the familiarity of discourse community members with both Arabic and French rhetoric has led to more tolerance for rhetorical transfer. Consequences of this transfer have also been outlined, including variation in modes of citation and the introduction of a more formal syllogistic type of argument in legal discourse. The chapter has also explored the tension-filled sociocultural climate surrounding *'iftaa'* as a means for better understanding the rhetorical patterns in fatwas and their variation and heterogeneity. The discussion indicates that the fatwas themselves contribute to the clash of ideologies and sociopolitical currents, eliciting sometimes vehement reactions from various social and cultural groups. This interaction between fatwas as a genre and elements of cultural context appears to have motivated diachronic changes concerning the purpose of the genre in particular. These changes need to be studied, using a theoretical framework such as Bhatia's *critical genre analysis* to detect unwarranted ideological manipulations. Finally, the chapter has presented a few remarks about generic practices and their cultural significance and outlined topics for further research that will enhance our understanding of Arabic genres.

Appendix A
COMPLETE REFERENCES OF FATWAS

LIST OF REFERENCES

1. Al-Ahmad, Mahmud Abdul Hameed. (2003). *Fataawaa tahummu almar'ataa lmu'aaSira* (Vol. 2) [Fatwas for Modern Women]. Beirut: Daar Alfikr Almu'aaSir.
2. Al-Moumni, Khalil. (1998). A*lfataawaa albadriyya* [Fatwas from Badr Mosque]. Casablanca: Daar Arrashaad AlHadiitha.
3. Qaradawi, Yusuf. (1981). *hudaa al'islaam: fatawaa mu'aaSira* (Vo1.1) [Guidance of Islam: Modern Fatwas]. Cairo: Daar Aafaaq Alghad.
4. Qaradawi, Yusuf. (1993). M*in hudaa al'islaam: fataawaa mu'aaSira* (Vol. 2) [Guidance of Islam: Modern Fatwas]. AlMansuriyya: Daar Alwafaa'.
5. Qaradawi, Yusuf. (2008). qaradawi.net.
6. Rifaa'ii, Qasim Shimaa'ii, ed. (1988). F*ataawaa 'islaamiyya* (Vol. 2 & 3) [Islamic Fatwas]. Beirut: Daar Al-Qalam.
7. Shawadfi, Safwat, ed. (1987). *Fataawaa hay'at kibaari al'ulamaa'* [Fatwas of the Council of Prominent Scholars]. Bilbays: Daar Attaqwaa.

LIST OF FATWAS

Mufti	Topic	Reference	Pages
Al-Ahmad	Profit margins	1	65
	Illegal incomes	1	67–68
	Down payments	1	70–71
	Late payment penalties	1	71–72
	Taxes	1	73–74
	Loan payment	1	75
Al-Moumni	Bribery	2	150
	Food imports	2	150–51
	Forbidden sales	2	164–65
	Bank loans	2	165–66
	Sale fraud	2	167–68
	Price markup	2	171
Committee	Intermediaries	6 (Vol. 3)	332–33
	Price markup	7	85–86
	Deferred payments	7	100–101

List of Fatwas (cont.)

Mufti	Topic	Reference	Pages
Ibn Baz	Trading in bank shares	6 (Vol. 2)	263–64
	Bank interest	6 (Vol. 2)	266–67
	Bank employment	6 (Vol. 2)	280–81
	Restaurant employment	6 (Vol. 3)	351
Qaradawi	Fixing wages by state	3	505–11
	Islam and commerce	3	520–25
	Bank employment	3	529–31
	Women employment	4	303–6
	Graphic design work	5	1–2
	Price fixing by state	5	1

Appendix B

COMPLETE REFERENCES OF COURT JUDGMENTS

LIST OF REFERENCES

1. Moroccan Supreme Court. 2006. *QaDaa'u almajlisi al'a'laa* [Judgments of The Supreme Court] (Vol. 64–65). Rabat: MaTba'at Al-Amiina.
2. Moroccan Supreme Court. 2006. *QaDaa'u almajlisi al'a'laa* [Judgments of The Supreme Court] (Vol. 66). Rabat: MaTba'at Al-Amiina.
3. *Al Milaf* [The File]. 2005. Number 5. Mohammadia: MaTba'at Fedala.
4. *Al Milaf* [The File]. 2005. Number 6. Mohammadia: MaTba'at Fedala.
5. *Al Milaf* [The File]. 2006. Number 9. Mohammadia: MaTba'at Fedala.

LIST OF COURT JUDGMENTS

Judgment #	Topic	Reference	Pages
	Social Chamber		
748	Employment contract	1	361–65
180	Illicit competition	1	370–72
214	Judicial fees	1	377–78
348	Work injury	1	384–88
524	Pensions	1	389–92
550	Family benefits	1	393–96
414	Power of attorney	2	321–26
415	Administrative procedure	2	327–30
424	Compensation for work accident	2	331–34
438	Employment termination	2	335–38
486	Work-related car accident	2	339–42
	Commerce Chamber		
715	Auctions	1	193–98
288	Debt declaration	1	228–31
374	Judicial liquidation	1	239–42
970	Abuse of authority	1	292–94
1202	Brokerage commission	2	141–44
295	Judicial guardianship	2	175–77
620	Company director's responsibility	2	207–9
702	Commercial rent	2	216–18
1004	Judicial liquidation and debts	2	247–50
1035	Bank–client relations	2	251–55
896	Error in judgment date	3	331–35
772	Court officer's report	4	353–58
288	Judicial liquidation and representation	4	359–61
913	Tenant eviction	5	309–13

Appendix C
FRENCH JUDGMENT

Cour de Cassation (Première Chambre Civile)
February 10, 1988

FRENCH ORIGINAL

LA COUR;—Sur le moyen unique: **Attendu que** M. Denis G . . . a été condamné pour tentative de meurtre sur la personne de son fils Josselin; **que** par la suite, son épouse a demandé à la juridiction civile de le déchoir de l'autorité parentale tant à l'égard de Josselin que sa soeur Aurélie; **que** l'arrêt attaqué (Caen, 27 mars 1986) a accueilli cette demande; **attendu que** M. G . . . fait grief à la cour d'appel d'avoir ainsi statué alors que, selon le moyen, au regard de l'art. 378-1 c. civ., seul applicable en l'espèce à l'exclusion de l'art. 378 du même code, la déchéance de l'autorité parentale suppose des exemples pernicieux de délinquance, ce qui implique une délinquance d'habitude ou, à tout le moins, des faits répétés; **que** des lors en se fondant, pour prononcer la déchéance, sur le fait unique ayant donné lieu à la condamnation pénale, la cour d'appel a violé les textes précités;

Mais **attendu que**, contrairement à ce que soutient le moyen, les juridictions civiles peuvent se fonder pour prononcer la déchéance de l'autorité parentale, non seulement sur les causes prévues par l'art. 378-1 c. civ., mais aussi sur celles de l'art. 378 de ce code lorsque la juridiction pénale n'a pas usé de la faculté qui lui était donnée de prononcer la déchéance; que le moyen n'est donc pas fondé;

Par ces motifs rejette . . .

TRANSLATION

THE COURT—Regarding the single plea; **considering that** Mr. Denis G. was sentenced for the attempted murder of his son Josselin; **that** subsequently his wife asked the civil court to remove his parental rights regarding both Josselin and his sister Aurélie; **that** the contested judgment (Caen, March 27, 1986) accepted this request—**considering that** Mr. G. held grievance against the court of appeals for so deciding even though, according to the plea and according to article 378-1 of the civil code, which is the only article applicable to the case to the exclusion of article 378 of the same code, the removal of parental rights presumes pernicious delinquency, which implies habitual delinquency or at least repeated acts; **that** by declaring the removal of parental rights on the basis of the single act that led to the sentence, the court of appeals violated the texts cited above;

But **considering that**, contrary to what the plea claims, civil jurisdictions may base their decisions for the removal of parental rights not only on the causes provided in article 378-1 of the civil code, but also on those of article 378 of this code when the penal court does not make use of the option available to it in order to declare the removal of parental rights; that therefore the plea is groundless.

For these reasons, rejects [the petitioner's plea to annul the appeals court's decision].

French Judgment

French original cited in R. Mendegris and G. Vermelle, 1996, *Le Commentaire d'Arrêt en Droit Privé*, Paris: Dalloz, p. 40 [Author's translation].

Appendix D

KEY ARABIC TERMS

'adab almufti: rules governing the conduct of muftis

'aalim: (plural: *'ulamaa'*) scholar, especially one who specializes in *sharii'a* and religious matters

alqawlu arraajiH: the preponderant opinion

aTTaalib (feminine: *aTTaaliba*): a person who petitions the court, for example, to invalidate an earlier judgment against him or her

aTTaa'in (feminine: *aTTaa'ina*): a person who contests the validity of a judgment before a court

daar al'iftaa': an institution that issues fatwas

fatwa: (plural: *fataawaa*) legal opinion based on *sharii'a* law

fiqh: Islamic law

fuqahaa': (singular: *faqiih*) Islamic jurists

hadith: narrative of the prophet's deeds and sayings

Hisba: traditional institution whose function is to control the price and quality of merchandise and weights and measures

'i'dhaar: notification of a litigant by a judge

'iftaa': the issuing of fatwas

imam: a person who leads prayers in a mosque

'isnaad: chain of transmission of hadith

'istiftaa': request for fatwas

madhhab: particular school of *sharii'a* law

mu'aamalaat: business transactions

mufti: a person who issues fatwas

mustafti: a person who seeks a mufti's legal opinion

muqallid: a mufti who simply gives the dominant opinion in a particular madhhab, a school thought in *sharii'a*

mustaqill: a mufti with sufficient credentials and scholarly preparation that enable him to use various methods of reasoning and provide independent opinions

naqD: decision by the Supreme Court that annuls a lower court's verdict

qaaDi: (Islamic) judge

qaDaa': (Islamic) judiciary

qiyaas: reasoning by analogy

rafD: decision by the Supreme Court that rejects a petitioner's request to annul a lower court decision against him

ribaa: usury

risaala: a legal essay

tajriid: the process of "stripping" fatwas by deleting details such as dates and names of people and places, for example, in order to extract the legal principle of the case so that it can be used to solve subsequent cases

talxiiS: summarizing fatwas

tanziil: legal method whereby the children of a person who dies before his father are entitled to inherit their father's share from their grandfather when the latter dies

tawliij: arrangements and transactions (e.g., sales and gifts) designed to circumvent the application of *sharii'a* laws of inheritance

'uSuul alfiqh: sources and methods of law

Appendix E

EXCERPTS IN ORIGINAL ARABIC SCRIPT

CHAPTER ONE

(1) لم يكن الفقهاء يتقيدون بالممكن الواقعي بل لقد ذهبوا مع الممكنات الذهنية إلى أبعد مدى مما جعل الفقه في الثقافات الإسلامية يقوم بذات الدور تقريبا الذي قامت به الرياضيات في الثقافة اليونانية والثقافة الأوروبية الحديثة ومن هنا أهميته بالنسبة للبحث الابستمولوجي في الثقافة الإسلامية وبالتالي بالنسبة للعقل العربي.

(2) وضوحا وجلاء

تتولد وتنشأ

(3) عارضوها في بعض الأحوال وأيدوها في أحوال أخرى وقيدو ها ببعض القيود في بعض الأحوال والتزموا حيالها سياسة الحياد في معظم الأحوال.

(4) يجب أن تحرر جميع التصرفات المتعلقة بنقل الملكية المشتركة أوإنشاء حقوق عينية عليها أو نقلها أو تعديلها أو إسقاطها بموجب محرررسمي أو محرر ثابت التاريخ يتم تحريره من طرف مهني ينتمي إلى مهنة قانونية ومنظمة يخولها قانونها تحرير العقود وذلك تحت طائلة الابطال.

CHAPTER THREE

(1) حيث يستفاد من وثائق الملف ومن القرار المطعون فيه . . . أن . . .

(2) حيث يؤخذ من عناصر الملف ومن القرار المطعون فيه . . . أن . . .

(3) وهذا هو القرار المطلوب نقضه من طرف الأجيرة.

(4) في شأن الفرع الأول للوسيلة الأولى حيث تنعى الطاعنة على القرار خرق الفصلين 452 . . . و345 . . . وفساد التعليل . . .

(5) حيث أثار المطلوب دفعا بعدم قبول الطلب لأن الطالب . . .

(6) فالمحكمة بتمسكها بعدم احترام الطاعنة لمقتضيات الفصل 12 تكون قدعللت قرارها تعليلا خاطئا ومخالفا للقانون مما يعرض القرار للنقض.

(7) حيث ثبتت صحة مانعاه الطاعن على القرار ذلك أن . . .

(8) . . . ذلك أن الفصل 6 من ظهير 2/6/1963 تعتبر في حكم حادثة الشغل الحادثة الطارئة للأجير بين مكان السكنى وبين مكان العمل وأن القرار المطعون فيه لما قضى بخلاف ذلك يكون غير مرتكز على أساس . . . مما يعرضه للنقض.

(9) . . . يكون القرار غير خارق لأي مقتضى ومعللا بما فيه الكفاية والوسيلة على غير أساس.

(10) قضى المجلس الأعلى برفض الطلب . . .

(11) قضى المجلس الأعلى بنقض القرار . . .

(12) في الشكل

حيث أن الاستئناف قدم داخل الأجل وتم وفق الشروط القانونية المتطلبة لقبولها شكلا . . .

في الجوهر

حيث يؤخذ من وثائق الملف . . .

(13) يجوز للإنسان أن يبيع سلعة . . . إلى أجل معلوم ولوزاد ثمن بيعها إلى أجل عن قيمتها وقت بيعها . . . لعموم قوله تعالى:" . . ." ولما ثبت عن النبي صلى الله عليه وسلم أنه قال:" . . ."

(14) - لايجوز بيع أسهم البنوك ولا شراؤها . . .
- لأنها مؤسسات ربوية لايجوز التعاون معها لقول الله سبحانه" . . ."
ولما ثبت عن النبي صلى الله عليه وسلم" . . ."

(15) - ووصيتي لك ولغيرك من المسلمين هو الحذر من جميع المعاملات الربوية والتحذير منها . . .
- إنني أرى أنه من المتعين علينا أن ندخل هذه المعركة العلمية التقنية بكل قوة . . .
- لكن مع الأسف الشديد المسلمون فقدوا الثقة من بعضهم بعضا وأصبحت معاملة المسلمين لبعضهم تعيش فوضى عارمة.

Excerpts in Original Arabic Script

(16) - النظام الاقتصادي في الإسلام يقوم على أساس محاربة الربا واعتباره من كبائر الذنوب.
- . . . ينهى عن استغلال التاجر للمشتري الجاهل سعر السلعة وهذا الشخص يسمى عند الفقهاء المسترسل.
- إن الشريعة الإسلامية تحرص على منع الضرر والضرار . . . وقد جاء في الحديث " لاضرر ولاضرار" . . . وقد رتب الفقهاء على هذه القاعدة فروعا شتى منها: أن الضرر يزال وأن الضرر لايزال بالضرر وأن الضرر الخاص يتحمل لدفع الضرر العام . . .

(17) وإذا أجزنا عمل المرأة فالواجب أن يكون مقيدا بعدة شروط . . .

(18) والقول بصحة بيع العربون هو أرجح القولين في المسألة لما في ذلك من تحقيق مصالح العباد وخاصة أنه لم يثبت النهي عن بيع العربون عن الرسول.

(19) لعن الله الخمر وشاربها وساقيها وعاصرها . . .

(20) وبصرف النظر عن بحث باقي الأوجه والوسيلة الأخرى . . .
قضى المجلس الأعلى بنقض وإبطال القرار المطعون فيه . . .

(22) أود أن أنبه هنا على حقيقة شرعية مهمة قد يغفل عنها كثير من الناس أويجهلونها . . .

(23) بناء على الأوراق الأخرى المدلى بها في الملف . . .

CHAPTER FOUR

(2) حيث يستفاد . . . أن . . .
حيث أنه . . .
حيث أن . . .
لهذه الأسباب
قضى المجلس بنقض . . .

(3) وأخضعت النازلة لمقتضيات المادة 419 من مدونة التجارة التي أعطت للمحكمة السلطة لتحديد أجرة السمسار إذا لم تحدد باتفاق أو عرف واستبعدت توصية جمعية الوكلاء العقاريين لولاية فاس المورخة في 20/5/01 لكونها لا ترقى إلى مرتبة القانون حتى يمكن اعتمادها كوثيقة لتحديد أجرة السمسار . . .

(4) إذا ترتب على توسط من شفع لك في الوظيفة حرمان من هو أولى وأحق بالتعيين فيها من جهة الكفاية العلمية التي تتعلق بها . . . فالشفاعة محرمة لأنها ظلم لمن هو أحق بها . . .

(5) وأجر المثل أو عوض المثل الذي ذكره فقهاؤنا يقصد به الأجر العادل الذي يستحقه مثله في مقابل عمله مع مراعاة كل الظروف والعوامل التي لها علاقة بتحديد قيمة العمل . . .

(6) . . . فقال له سعد: يا أخي إنني من أكثر الناس أموالا فتعالى أشاطرك مالي وعندي زوجتان أنظر إلى أوقعها في قلبك أطلقها لك . . . وعندي داران تسكن إحداهما وأنا أسكن الأخرى قال له: يا أخي بارك الله لك في مالك وفي أهلك وفي دارك إنني أنا امرؤ تاجر فدلوني على السوق.

(8) زوج المرأة الفرنسية الذي دخل القسم

(15) الدائن المرتهن الذي ينبغي إشعاره من طرف مالك العقار بالرغبةفي فسخ عقد الكراء

(16) يعيب الطاعن على القرار المطعون فيه تحريف منحة الاقدمية.

(17) يعيب الطاعن على القرار المطعون فيه أنه حرف منحة الاقدمية.

(18) لايجوز العمل في مثل هذه البنوك . . .

(19) لايجوز لك أن تعمل في محلات تبيع الخمور . . .

Chapter Number

(20) يجوز للإنسان أن يبيع سلعة . . .

(21) - المادة 419 من مدونة التجارة

- سوء تطبيق مقتضيات المادة 419 من مدونة التجارة.

(22) يعيب الطاعن على القرار المطعون فيه . . . سوء ونقصان التعليل الموازي لانعدامه.

(23) إن الدعوى التي أقامتها المطلوبة تهدف إلى الحكم على البنك بأدائها لها تعويضا عن الضرر الذي تسبب فيه لها بعدم تقديمه الكمبيالات المسلمة له للاستخلاص في آجالها المحددة.

(24) - التعاون على الإثم والعدوان

- وتعاونوا على البر والتقوى ولا تعاونوا على الإثم والعدوان.

(25) - الأمر بالمعروف والنهي عن المنكر

- المؤمنون والمؤمنات بعضهم أولياء بعض يأمرون بالمعروف وينهون عن المنكر.

(26) - بيع المسلم على المسلم

- لايبع بعضكم على بيع بعض.

(27) حرم الإسلام كل مظهر من مظاهر التعاون على الإثم والعدوان.

Appendix F

VERSIONS OF A MODIFIED FATWA USED IN THE STUDY OF THE EFFECT OF SOURCES ON THE PERCEIVED QUALITY OF FATWAS

FATWA VERSION 1

السؤال: إذا اشترى إنسان سلعة من مخزن أو دكان وعدها عليه صاحبها بأعيانها فهل يبيعها المشتري بعد عدها واستلامها أو لابد من أن يحوزها وينقلها إلى محل آخر؟

الجواب: إذا اشترى إنسان سلعة من مخزن أو دكان وعدها عليه صاحبها بأعيانها فلا يجوز للمشتري أن يبيعها في محلها بمجرد عدد أعيانها ولا يعتبر ذلك تسلما بل لابد لجواز بيع المشتري لها من حوزه إياها إلى محل آخر وذلك لما جاء في الأحاديث التالية:

- "إذا اشتريت شيئا فلا تبعه حتى تقبضه."
- "نهى النبي أن تباع السلع حيث تبتاع حتى يحوزها التجار إلى رحالهم."
- "إذا ابتعت طعاما فلا تبعه حتى تستوفيه."
- "من ابتاع طعاما فلا يبيعه حتى يكتاله."

Translation:

Question: If a person purchases some merchandise from a store and the seller presents it to him, can the buyer resell the merchandise then or does he have to take possession of it and move it to another location first?

Answer: If a person purchases some merchandise from a store and the seller presents it to him, the buyer is not allowed to resell it where he has received it, but must take possession of it and move it to another location first because of the following hadiths:

— "If you purchase something, do not sell it until you get hold of it."
— "The prophet prohibited the resale of a merchandise where it was bought; the merchants must first join it to their possessions."
— "If you purchase food, do not sell it until you receive it in its totality."
— "Whoever purchases food should not sell it until he obtains it."

FATWA VERSION 2

السؤال: إذا اشترى إنسان سلعة من مخزن أو دكان وعدها عليه صاحبها بأعيانها فهل يبيعها المشتري بعد عدها واستلامها أو لابد من أن يحوزها وينقلها إلى محل آخر؟

الجواب: إذا اشترى إنسان سلعة من مخزن أو دكان وعدها عليه صاحبها بأعيانها فلا يجوز للمشتري أن يبيعها في محلها بمجرد عدد أعيانها ولا يعتبر ذلك تسلما بل لابد لجواز بيع المشتري لها من حوزه إياها إلى محل آخر لما رواه أحمد رحمه الله عن حكيم بن حزام أن رسول الله صلى الله عليه وسلم قال: "إذا اشتريت شيئا فلا تبعه حتى تقبضه." ولما رواه أحمد وأبو داوود عن زيد بن ثابت رضي الله عنه

أن النبي صلى الله عليه وسلم: "نهى أن تباع السلع حيث تبتاع حتى يحوزها التجار إلى رحالهم." ولما رواه أحمد ومسلم عن جابر رضي الله عنه انه قال: قال النبي صلى الله عليه وسلم: "إذا ابتعت طعاما فلا تبعه حتى تستوفيه." وفي رواية لمسلم أن النبي صلى الله عليه وسلم قال: "من ابتاع طعاما فلا يبيعه حتى يكتاله."

Translation:

Question: If a person purchases some merchandise from a store and the seller presents it to him, can the buyer resell the merchandise then or does he have to take possession of it and move it to another location first?

Answer: If a person purchases some merchandise from a store and the seller presents it to him, the buyer is not allowed to resell it where he has received it, but must take possession of it and move it to another location because of what was reported by Ahmad may God have mercy upon him from Hakim Ibn Hizaam that the messenger of God may God's blessing and peace be upon him said: "If you purchase something, do not sell it until you get hold of it." And because of what was reported by Ahmad and Abu Daawuud from Zayd Ibn Thaabit may God be pleased with him that the prophet may God's blessing and peace be upon him "prohibited the resale of merchandise where it was bought; they must first join it to their possessions." And because of what was reported by Ahmad and Muslim from Jaabir may God be pleased with him, who said: The prophet may God's blessing and peace be upon him said: "If you purchase food, do not sell it until you receive in its totality." And in a report by Muslim, the prophet may God's blessing and peace be upon him said: "Whoever purchases food should not sell it until he obtains it."

REFERENCES[1]

Ahmad, Ummul. 1997. Research Article Introductions in Malay: Rhetoric in an Emerging Research Community. In *Culture and Styles in Academic Discourse,* ed. A. Duszak, 273–303. Berlin: De Gruyter.

Aijmer, Karin. 2007. Idiomaticity in a Cultural Activity Type Perspective: The Conventionalization of Routine Phrases in Answering-Machine Messages. In *Phraseology and Culture in English,* ed. P. Skandera, 323–49. Berlin and New York: Mouton de Gruyter.

Alabboudi, Abdelali. 1986. *Majmuu'atu al'aHkaami ashshar'iyya by Al-Hassan Ben Al-Haj Mohammad Laamaarti* [Collection of Islamic Court Judgments issued by Al-Hassan Ben Al-Haj Mohammad Laamaarti]. Casablanca: Arab Cultural Center.

Al-Batal, Mahmoud. 1990. Connectives as Cohesive Elements in a Modern Expository Arabic Text. In *Perspectives on Arabic Linguistics II,* ed. M. Eid and J. McCarthy, 234–68. Amsterdam and Philadelphia: John Benjamins.

Al-Hajoui, Mohamed. 2005. *atta'aaDudu almatiin bayna al'aqli wa al'ilmi wa addiin* [Solid Mutual Support between Reason, Science, and Religion]. Ed. Mohamed Benazzouz. Beirut: Daar Ibn Hazm.

Al-Jabri, Mohamed. 2003. *takwiinu al'aqli al'arabii* [The Formation of the Arab Mind]. Casablanca: daaru annashr.

Al-Jubouri, Adnan. 1983. The Role of Repetition in Arabic Argumentative Discourse. In *English for Specific Purposes in the Arab World,* ed. J. Swales and H. Mustapha, 99–117. Birmingham, UK: University of Aston.

Al-Khawarizmi, Mohamed Ibn Musa. 1968. *Kitaabu aljabri wa almuqaabala* [The Book on Restoration and Balancing]. Cairo: Daar Alkitaabi Al'arabii.

Al Milaf. 2003. Issue 1. Casablanca: Matba'at Annajaah Al-Jadiida.

Al Milaf. 2005. Issue 6. Mohammadia: MaTba'at Fedala.

Al-Wanshariisii, Ahmad Ibn Yahya. 1981/1983. *Al-Mi'yaar.* Rabat: Ministry of Culture and Religious Affairs.

Arent, Russell. 1998. The Pragmatics of Cross-Cultural Bargaining in an Amman Suq: An Exploration of Language Choice, Discourse Structure and Pragmatic Failure in Discourse Involving Arab and Non-Arab Participants (Jordan, Amman). PhD diss., University of Minnesota.

Atkinson, Dwight. 1999. TESOL and Culture. *TESOL Quarterly* 33: 625–54.

———. 2003. Writing and Culture in the Post-process Era. *Journal of Second Language Writing* 12: 49–63.

Bakhtin, Michael. 1986. *Speech Genres and Other Essays.* Austin: University of Texas Press.

Barthes, Roland. 1977. *Image, Music, Text.* Trans. Stephen Heath. New York: Hill & Wang.

1. Complete references to the Fatwas and the Court Judgments are given in Appendix A and Appendix B, respectively.

Bassiouney, Reem. 2009. *Arabic Sociolinguistics: Topics in Diglossia, Gender, Identity, and Politics.* Washington, DC: Georgetown University Press.

Bentahila, Abdelali, and Eirlys Davies. 1983. The Syntax of Arabic-French Code-Switching. *Lingua* 59: 301–30.

———. 1992. Code-Switching and Language Dominance. In *Cognitive Processing in Bilinguals,* ed. R. J. Harris, 443–58. Amsterdam: Elsevier.

———. 2002. Language Mixing in Rai Music: Localisation or Globalisation? *Language & Communication* 22: 187–207.

Bhatia, Vijay. 1983. Simplification v. Easification: The Case of Legal Texts. *Applied Linguistics* 4: 42–54.

———. 1992. Pragmatics of the Use of Nominals in Academic and Professional Genres. In *Pragmatics and Language Learning,* ed. L. Bouton and Y. Kashru, 217–30. Urbana-Champaign: University of Illinois.

———. 1993. *Analysing Genre: Language Use in Professional Settings.* London: Longman.

———. 2008. Towards Critical Genre Analysis. In *Advances in Discourse Studies,* ed. V. K. Bhatia, J. Flowerdew, and R. H. Jones, 166–77. London and New York: Routledge.

Blanc, Haim. 1960. Style Variation in Spoken Arabic: A Sample of Interdialectal Educated Conversation. In *Contributions to Arabic Linguistics,* ed. Charles Ferguson. Cambridge, MA: Harvard University Press.

Block, David. 1996. Not So Fast: Some Thoughts on Theory Culling, Relativism, Accepted Findings and the Heart and Soul of SLA. *Applied Linguistics* 17 (1): 63–83.

Brown, Gillian, and George Yule. 1988. *Discourse Analysis.* Cambridge: Cambridge University Press.

Charles, Maggie. 2009. Stance, Interaction and the Rhetorical Patterning of Restrictive Adverbs: Discourse Roles of *Only, Just, Simply,* and *Merely.* In *Academic Writing: At the Interface of Corpus and Discourse,* ed. M. Charles, 152–69. London: Continuum International.

Clerehan, Rosemary, and Rachelle Buchbinder. 2006. Toward a More Valid Account of Functional Text Quality: The Case of the Patient Information Leaflet. *Text and Talk* 26 (1): 39–68.

Conley, John, and William O'Barr. 2005. *Just Words: Law, Language, and Power.* Chicago: University of Chicago Press.

Connor, Ulla. 1996. *Contrastive Rhetoric.* Cambridge: Cambridge University Press.

———. 2002. New Directions in Contrastive Rhetoric. *TESOL Quarterly* 36: 493–510.

Cornu, Gérard. 1990. *Linguistique Juridique.* Paris: Montchrestien.

Coulmas, Florian, ed. 1981. *Conversational Routine: Explorations in Standardized Communication Situations and Pre-patterned Speech.* The Hague; Paris; New York: Mouton.

Cowie, Anthony, ed. 1998. *Phraseology.* Oxford: Clarendon Press.

Davies, Bethan. 2007. Grice's Cooperative Principle: Meaning and Rationality. *Journal of Pragmatics* 39: 2308–31.

DePalma, Michael-John, and Jeffrey Ringer. 2011. Toward a Theory of Adaptive Transfer: Expanding Disciplinary Discussions of "Transfer" in Second Language Writing and Composition Studies. *Journal of Second Language Writing* 20: 134–47.

Devitt, Amy. 1989. Genre as Textual Variable: Some Historical Evidence from Scots and American English. *American Speech* 64: 291–303.
———. 2004. *Writing Genres.* Carbondale: Southern Illinois University Press.
Duszak, Anna. 1994. Academic Discourse and Intellectual Styles. *Journal of Pragmatics* 24: 291–313.
Eid, Mushira. 1988. Principles for Switching between Standard and Egyptian Arabic. *Al-'Arabiyya* 21: 51–80.
———. 1990. Arabic Linguistics: The Current Scene. In *Perspectives on Arabic Linguistics I,* ed. M. Eid, 3–37. Amsterdam and Philadelphia: John Benjamins.
———. 2002. Language Is Choice: Variation in Egyptian Women's Written Discourse. In *Language Contact and Language Conflict in Arabic,* ed. A. Rouchdy, 203–32. London: Routledge Curzon.
Fakhri, Ahmed. 1994. Text Organization and Transfer: The Case of Arab ESL Learners. *International Review of Applied Linguistics* 4(1): 78–86.
———. 1995. Topic Continuity in Arabic Narrative Discourse. In *Perspectives on Arabic Linguistics VII,* ed. M. Eid, 141–55. Amsterdam and Philadelphia: John Benjamins.
———. 1998. Reported Speech in Arabic Journalistic Discourse. In *Perspectives on Arabic Linguistics XI,* ed. E. Benmamoun, M. Eid, and N. Haeri, 167–82. Amsterdam and Philadelphia: John Benjamins.
———. 2002. Borrowing Discourse Patterns: French Rhetoric in Arabic Legal Texts. In *Perspectives on Arabic Linguistics XIV,* ed. D. Parkinson and E. Benmamoun, 155–70. Amsterdam and Philadelphia: John Benjamins.
———. 2004. Rhetorical Properties of Arabic Research Article Introductions. *Journal of Pragmatics* 36: 1119–38.
———. 2005. Discourse Analysis. In *Encyclopedia of Arabic Language and Linguistics I,* ed. K. Versteegh, 364–65. Leiden: Brill Academic.
———. 2008. Citations in Arabic Legal Opinion. In *Perspectives on Arabic Linguistics XXI,* ed. D. Parkinson, 115–31. Amsterdam and Philadelphia: John Benjamins.
———. 2009. Rhetorical Variation in Arabic Academic Discourse: Humanities versus Law. *Journal of Pragmatics* 41: 306–24.
———. 2012a. Nominalization in Arabic Discourse: A Genre Analysis Perspective. In *Arabic Language and Linguistics,* ed. R. Bassiouney and E. G. Katz, 145–55. Washington, DC: Georgetown University Press.
———. 2012b. An Empirical Study of the Effect of *'isnaad* on the Perceived Quality of *'iftaa'.* Paper read at the 65th Annual Kentucky Foreign Language Conference, University of Kentucky, Lexington, April.
Farquhar, Neil. 2009. Fatwa Online, April 21. http://baithak.blogspot.com/2009/04/fatwa-online-neil-farquhar.html
Ferguson, Charles. 1959. Diglossia. *Word* 15: 325–40.
Feteris, Eveline. 1999. *Fundamentals of Legal Argumentation.* Dordrecht: Kluwer Academic.
Flowerdew, John. 2000. Discourse Communities, Legitimate Peripheral Participation, and the Nonnative-English-Speaking Scholar. *TESOL Quarterly* 34: 127–50.
Flowerdew, John, and Alina Wan. 2010. The Linguistic and the Contextual in Applied Genre Analysis: The Case of the Company Audit Report. *English for Specific Purposes* 29: 78–93.

Foucault, Michel. 1984. What Is an Author? In *The Foucault Reader*, ed. P. Robonow, 101–20. New York: Pantheon Books.

Freedman, Aviva, and Peter Medway, eds. 1994. *Genre and the New Rhetoric*. London: Taylor and Francis.

Gibbons, John, ed. 1994. *Language and the Law*. London and New York: Longman.

Givón, Talmy. 1983. *Topic Continuity in Discourse: A Quantitative Cross-Cultural Study*. Amsterdam and Philadelphia: John Benjamins.

———. 2009. *The Genesis of Syntactic Complexity*. Amsterdam and Philadelphia: John Benjamins.

Goffman, Erving. 1981. *Forms of Talk*. Philadelphia: University of Philadelphia Press.

Grice, Paul. 1991. Logic and Conversation. In *Pragmatics: A Reader*, ed. S. Davis, 305–15. New York and Oxford: Oxford University Press.

Guichard, Pierre, and Manuela Marin. 1995. Avant Propos. In *Histoire et Société en Occident Musulman au Moyen Age: Analyse du Mi'yaar d'Al-Wanshariisii*, ed. V. Lagardère, 7–15. Madrid: Consejo Superior De Investigationes Cientificas.

Gumperz, John. 1971. *Language in Social Groups*. Ed. A. Dil. Palo Alto, CA: Stanford University Press.

———. 1982. *Language and Social Identity*. Cambridge: Cambridge University Press.

Gumperz, John, and Dell Hymes. 1972. *Directions in Sociolinguistics: The Ethnography of Communication*. New York: Holt, Reinhart, and Winston.

Haddad, Yvonne. 1996. Operation Desert Storm and the War of Fatwas. In *Islamic Legal Interpretation*, ed. M. Masud, B. Messick, and D. Powers, 297–309. Cambridge, MA: Harvard University Press.

Hallaq, Wael. 2001. *Authority, Continuity, and Change in Islamic Law*. Cambridge: Cambridge University Press.

———. 2005. *The Origins and Evolution of Islamic Law*. Cambridge: Cambridge University Press.

Halliday, Michael. 1994. *An Introduction to Functional Grammar*. London: Edward Arnold.

Halliday, Michael, and Ruqaiya Hasan. 1989. *Language, Context and Text: Aspects of Language in a Social-Semiotic Perspective*. Oxford: Oxford University Press.

Harding, Jeremy. 2009. Fatwa Shopping. http://www.lrb.co.uk/blog/2009/12/08/jeremy-harding/fatwa-shopping

Hasan, Ruqaiya. 1989. The Identity of a Text. In *Language, Context and Text: Aspects of Language in a Social-Semiotic Perspective*, ed. M. A. K. Halliday and R. Hasan, 97–116. Oxford: Oxford University Press.

Hatim, Basil. 1997. *Communication Across Cultures: Translation Theory and Contrastive Text Linguistics*. Exeter, UK: University of Exeter Press.

Heath, Jeffrey. 1989. *From Code-Switching to Borrowing: Foreign and Diglossic Mixing in Moroccan Arabic*. London and New York: Kegan Paul International.

Heyd, Uriel. 1969. Some Aspects of the Ottoman Fetva. *Bulletin of the School of Oriental and African Studies* 32: 35–56.

Hickey, Francesca, and Koenraad Kuiper. 2000. A Deep Depression Covers the South Tasman Sea: New Zealand Met Office Weather Forecasts. In *New Zealand English,* ed. A. Bell and K. Kuiper, 279–96. Amsterdam: John Benjamins.

Hinds, John. 1987. Reader Versus Writer Responsibility: A New Typology. In *Writing Across Languages: Analysis of L2 Text,* ed. U. Connor and R. Kaplan, 141–52. Reading, MA: Addison-Wesley.

Holes, Clive. 1984. *Colloquial Arabic of the Gulf and Saudi Arabia.* London: Routledge & Kegan Paul.

———. 2004. *Modern Arabic: Structures, Functions, and Varieties.* Washington, DC: Georgetown University Press.

Hopper, Paul. 1979. Aspect and Foregrounding in Discourse. In *Syntax and Semantics 12: Discourse and Syntax,* ed. T. Givón, 213–41. New York: Academic Press.

Hyland, Ken. 2000. *Disciplinary Discourses: Social Interactions in Academic Writing.* London: Longman.

———. 2003. Genre-Based Pedagogies: A Social Response to Process. *Journal of Second Language Writing* 12: 17–29.

———. 2007. *Genre and Second Language Writing.* Ann Arbor: University of Michigan Press.

Hyland, Ken, and Polly Tse. 2005. Hooking the Reader: A Corpus Study of Evaluative *that* in Abstracts. *English for Specific Purposes* 24: 123–39.

Hymes, Dell. 1964. *Language in Culture and Society: A Reader in Linguistics and Anthropology.* New York: Harper & Row.

Hyon, Sunny. 1996. Genre in Three Traditions: Implications for ESL. *TESOL Quarterly* 30: 693–722.

Ibn Khaldun. 1958. *The Muqaddimah: An Introduction to History.* Vol. 2. Trans. F. Rosenthal. New York: Pantheon Books.

Ibn Taymiyya, Taqi Din. 2002. *Alfataawaa alkubraa.* Beirut: daaru alkutub al'ilmiyya.

Ibn Uthaymiin, Muhammad Salah. n.d. *Duruus wa fataawaa fii alHarami almakkii* [Lectures and Fatwas in the Sacred Mecca Mosque]. Riyad: Maktabat Shams.

Institut Supérieur de la Magistrature. 2009. http://www.ism.ma.

Jackendoff, Ray. 2002. *Foundations of Language: Brain, Meaning, Grammar, Evolution.* Oxford: Oxford University Press.

Jakobson, Roman. 1960. Closing Statement: Linguistics and Poetics. In *Style in Language,* ed. T. Sebeok, 350–77. Cambridge, MA: MIT Press.

Jogthong, Chalermsi. 2001. Research Article Introductions in Thai: Genre Analysis of Academic Writing. EdD Diss., West Virginia University.

Johns, Ann, ed. 2002. *Genre and Pedagogy: Multiple Perspectives.* Mahwah, NJ: Lawrence Erlbaum.

Johnstone, Barbara. 1990. Orality and Discourse Structure in Modern Standard Arabic. In *Perspectives on Arabic Linguistics I,* ed. M. Eid, 215–33. Amsterdam and Philadelphia: John Benjamins.

———. 1991. *Repetition in Arabic Discourse.* Amsterdam and Philadelphia: John Benjamins.

Kaplan, Abraham. 1963. *The Conduct of Inquiry: Methodology for Behavioral Science.* New York: Harper and Row.

Keenan, Elinor Ochs. 1976. The Universality of Conversational Postulates. *Language in Society* 5: 67–80.
Khalil, Esam. 2000. *Grounding in English and Arabic News Discourse.* Amsterdam and Philadelphia: John Benjamins.
Kharraki, Abdennour. 2001. Moroccan Sex-based Differences in Bargaining. *Discourse & Society* 12(5): 615–25.
Koch, Barbara. 1983. Presentation as Proof: The Language of Arabic Rhetoric. *Anthropological Linguistics* 25(1): 47–60.
Kubota, Ryuko, and Al Lehner. 2004. Toward Critical Contrastive Rhetoric. *Journal of Second Language Writing* 13: 7–37.
Kuiper, Koenraad. 1996. *Smooth Talkers: The Linguistic Performance of Auctioneers and Sports casters.* Mahwah, NJ: Lawrence Erlbaum.
Kuiper, Koenraad, and Paddy Austin. 1990. They're Off and Racing Now: The Speech of the New Zealander Race Caller. In *New Zealand Ways of Speaking English,* ed. A. Bell and J. Holmes, 195–220. Clevedon: Multilingual Matters.
Labov, William. 1972. *Language in the Inner City.* Philadelphia: University of Pennsylvania Press.
Lagardère, Vincent. 1995. *Histoire et Société en Occident Musulman au Moyen Âge: Analyse du Mi'yaar d' Al-Wanshariisii.* Madrid: Consejo Superior De Investigationes Cientificas.
Lamine, Omar. 2005. al'amalu al qaDaa'ii almaghribii fii alqaDaayaa allatii lam yunaSS 'alayhaa fii mudawwanati al'aHwaali ashshaxSiyya [Moroccan Judicial Work on Cases Not Stipulated in the Code of Personal Status.] Doctoral Diss., Daar Al-Hadith Al-Hassaniyya.
Lasser, Mitchel de S-O. 1995. Judicial (Self-) Portraits: Judicial Discourse in the French Legal System. *The Yale Law Journal* 104(6): 1325–410.
Latour, Bruno. 1987. *Science in Action.* Cambridge, MA: Harvard University Press.
Levinson, Stephen. 1983. *Pragmatics.* Cambridge: Cambridge University Press.
Lindblom, Kenneth. 2001. Cooperating with Grice: A Cross-Disciplinary Metaperspective on Uses of Grice's Cooperative Principle. *Journal of Pragmatics* 33: 1601–23.
Loi, Chek Kim, and Moyra Sweetnam Evans. 2010. Cultural Differences in the Organization of Research Article Introductions from the Field of Educational Psychology: English and Chinese. *Journal of Pragmatics* 42: 2814–25.
Maley, Yon. 1987. The Language of Legislation. *Language in Society* 16: 25–48.
Mallat, Chibli. 1996. Tantawi on Banking Operations in Egypt. In *Islamic Legal Interpretation,* ed. M. Masud, B. Messick, and D. Powers, 286–96. Cambridge, MA: Harvard University Press.
Masud, Khalid. 1984. 'Adab al-Mufti: The Muslim Understanding of Values, Characteristics, and Role of a Mufti. In *Moral Conduct and Authority: The Place of Adab in South Asian Islam,* ed. B. Metcalf, 124–50. Berkley: University of California Press.
Masud, Khalid, Brinkley Messick, and David Powers. 1996. *Islamic Legal Interpretation: Muftis and Their Fatwas.* Cambridge, MA: Harvard University Press.
Mattila, Heikki. 2006. *Comparative Legal Linguistics.* Burlington, VT: Ashgate.

Meddeb, Abdelwahab. 2003. *The Malady of Islam.* Trans. from French by P. Jorisand A. Reid. New York: Basic Books.
Mendegris, Roger, and George Vermelle. 1996. *Le Commentaire d'Arrêt en Droit Privé.* Paris: Dalloz.
Messick, Brinkley. 1996. Media Muftis: Radio Fatwas in Yemen. In *Islamic Legal Interpretation,* ed. M. Masud, B. Messick, and D. Powers, 310–20. Cambridge, MA: Harvard University Press.
Miller, Carolyn. 1984. Genre as Social Action. *Quarterly Journal of Speech* 70: 151–67.
Mitchell, Terrence. 1986. What Is Educated Spoken Arabic? *International Journal of the Sociology of Language* 61: 7–32.
Majallat alqaDaa' wa alqaanuun. 1989. Numbers 140–41. Casablanca: Daar Annashr.
Moroccan Supreme Court. 1999. *Al'aHkaamu aSSaadiratu 'an majlisi al'isti'naafi ashshar'ii al'a'laa* [Judgments issued by the supreme *sharii'a* court of appeals]. Vol. 1. Mohammadia: MaTba'at Fedala.
Moumen, Mohamed. 2000. *ashsharTu al'ittifaaqii bi'adami almunaafasa fii 'aqdi ashshughl.* [Agreement Clause in Employment Contracts Prohibiting Competition]. *Majallat alqaDaa' wa alqaanuun* 18:11–49.
Mudawwanatu Al'usra. 2008. [Moroccan Family Code]. Imprimerie Rabat Net Maroc: Rabat.
Najjar, Hazem. 1990. Arabic as a Research Language: The Case of Agricultural Sciences. PhD Diss., University of Michigan.
Ochs, Elinor. 1997. Narrative. In *Discourse as Structure and Process,* ed. T. vanDijk, 185–207. London: Sage.
Omar, Margaret. 1976. *Levantine and Egyptian Arabic: A Comparative Study.* Washington, DC: Foreign Service Institute.
Owens, Johnathan, and Trent Rockwood. 2008. *Ya'ni:* What It (Really) Means. In *Perspectives on Arabic Linguistics XXI,* ed. D. Parkinson, 83–113. Amsterdam and Philadelphia: John Benjamins.
Paltridge, Brian. 1997. *Genre, Frames and Writing in Research Settings.* Amsterdam and Philadelphia: John Benjamins.
———. 2001. *Genre and the Language Learning Classroom.* Ann Arbor: University of Michigan Press.
Pawley, Andrew. 2007. Developments in the Study of Formulaic Language Since 1970: A Personal View. In *Phraseology and Culture in English,* ed. P. Skandera, 3–45. Berlin and New York: Mouton de Gruyter.
Penman, Robyn. 1987. Discourse in Courts: Cooperation, Coercion, and Coherence. *Discourse Processes* 10: 201–18.
Pennycook, Alastair. 1994. *The Cultural Politics of English as an International Language.* London: Longman.
———. 1996. Borrowing Others' Words: Text Ownership, Memory, and Plagiarism. *TESOL Quarterly* 30: 201–31.
Perleman, Chaim, and Lucie Olbrechts-Tyteca. 1969. *The New Rhetoric: A Treatise on Argumentation.* Notre Dame: University of Notre Dame Press.
Phillips, Nelson, and Cynthia Hardy. 2002. *Discourse Analysis: Investigating Processes of Social Construction.* London: Sage.
Pinker, Steven. 1997. *How the Mind Works.* New York: Norton.

———. 2007. *The Stuff of Thought: Language as a Window on Human Nature.* New York: Viking.

Polio, Charlene, and Ling Shi. 2012. Perceptions and Beliefs about Textual Appropriation and Source Use in Second Language Writing. *Journal of Second Language Writing* 21: 95–101.

Powers, David. 1990. A Court Case from Fourteenth-Century North Africa. *Journal of the American Oriental Society* 110(2): 229–54.

———. 2002. *Law, Society, and Culture in the Maghrib, 1300–1500.* Cambridge: Cambridge University Press.

Roy, Oliver. 2004. *Globalized Islam: The Search for a New Ummah.* New York: Columbia University Press.

Sa'adeddin, Mohamed. 1989. Text Development and Arabic-English Negative Interference. *Applied Linguistics* 10: 36–51.

Senturk, Recep. 2005. *Narrative Social Structure: Anatomy of Hadith Transmission Network, 610–1505.* Stanford, CA: Stanford University Press.

Sériaux, Alain. 1997. *Le Commentaire de Textes Juridiques: Arrêts et Jugements.* Paris: Ellipses.

Skandera, Paul, ed. 2007. *Phraseology and Culture in English.* Berlin and New York: Mouton de Gruyter.

Spack, Ruth. 1997. The Rhetorical Construction of Multilingual Students. *TESOL Quarterly* 31: 765–74.

Starck, Boris. 1972. *Droit Civil: Obligations.* Paris: Librairies Techniques.

Stroller, Fredrika, and Martin Robinson. 2013. Chemistry Journal Articles: An Interdisciplinary Approach to Move Analysis with Pedagogical Aims. *English for Specific Purposes* 32: 45–57.

Swales, John. 1981. *Aspects of Article Introductions.* Birmingham, UK: University of Aston.

———. 1990. *Genre Analysis: English in Academic and Research Settings.* Cambridge: Cambridge University Press.

———. 2004. *Research Genres: Explorations and Applications.* Cambridge: Cambridge University Press.

Swales, John, and Hazem Najjar. 1987. The Writing of Research Article Introductions. *Written Communication* 4: 175–92.

Tadros, Angele. 1993. The Pragmatics of Text Averral and Attribution in Academic Texts. In *Data, Description, Discourse,* ed. M. Hoey, 98–114. London: Harper Collins.

Taylor, Gordon, and Tingguang Chen. 1991. Linguistic, Cultural, and Subcultural Issues in Contrastive Discourse Analysis: Anglo-American and Chinese Scientific Texts. *Applied Linguistics* 12: 106–28.

Thomas, J. 2001. Conversational Maxims. In *Concise Encyclopedia of Sociolinguistics,* ed. R. Mesthrie, 116–21. Amsterdam: Elsevier.

Thompson, Geoff, and Ye Yiyun. 1991. Evaluation in the Reporting Verbs Used in Academic Papers. *Applied Linguistics* 12(4): 365–82.

Tibi, Bassam. 2001. *Islam between Culture and Politics.* New York: Palgrave.

Tiersma, Peter. 1999. *Legal Language.* Chicago: University of Chicago Press.

Toulmin, Stephen. 1958. *The Uses of Argument.* Cambridge: Cambridge University Press.

United Nations Development Fund for Women. 2004. *Progress of Arab Women 2004.* http://www.unifem.org/materials/item_detail4863.html.

Van Dijk, Teun. 1996. Discourse, Power and Access. In *Texts and Practices,* ed. C. Caldas-Coulthard and M. Coulthard, 84–104. London: Routledge.
van Eemeren, Frans et al. 1997. Argumentation. In *Discourse as Structure and Process,* ed. T. van Dijk, 208–29. London: Sage.
Vogel, Frank. 1996. The Complementarity of *'Iftaa'* and *QaDaa'*: Three Saudi Fatwas on Divorce. In *Islamic Legal Interpretation,* ed. M. Masud, B. Messick, and D. Powers, 262–69. Cambridge, MA: Harvard University Press.
Weinert, Regina. 1995. The Role of Formulaic Language in Second Language Acquisition: A Review. *Applied Linguistics* 16(2): 180–205.
Wray, Alison, and Kazuhiko Namba. 2003. Use of Formulaic Language by a Japanese–English Bilingual Child: A Practical Approach to Data Analysis. *Japanese Journal for Multilingualism* and *Multiculturalism* 9(1): 24–51.
Wray, Alison, and Michael Perkins. 2000. The Functions of Formulaic Language: An Integrated Model. *Language & Communication* 20: 1–28.
Zamel, Vivian. 1997. Toward a Model of Transculturation. *TESOL Quarterly* 31: 341–52.

INDEX OF NAMES

INDEX OF SUBJECTS

CPSIA information can be obtained
at www.ICGtesting.com
Printed in the USA
BVHW030051081121
621028BV00012B/204